FRONTIERS
IN
MODERN THEOLOGY

FRONTIERS
IN
MODERN THEOLOGY

by
Carl F. H. Henry

WITHDRAWN

MOODY PRESS
CHICAGO

CONTENTS

Foreword

THE APPEARANCE in *Christianity Today* of this series of essays on current theological trends created an interest beyond my fondest hopes. Scholars familiar with the European religious scene took time to write, mostly in a highly appreciative way. Trinity Evangelical Divinity School in Bannockburn, Illinois, invited me to present this theological assessment in December of 1964 to an alert student body. Simultaneously with its appearance in the magazine, Winona Lake School of Theology invited me to devote the G. Campbell Morgan lecture series in the summer of 1965 to the same theme. The material held an attraction for seminarians on many campuses, and their frequently voiced hope that the content might be available in more permanent form is hereby fulfilled through the interest of the publishers of this volume.

It was highly gratifying, in fact, to discover the lively interest of editors on both sides of the Atlantic in this series of essays. The religion editor of *Time* magazine wrote to indicate his personal interest in the series. From London came a request from the Victoria Institute (Philosophical Society of Great Britain) asking permission to reprint the series for British readers in the society's annual magazine, *Faith and Thought,* in the spring of 1965. This present paperback volume, however, adds additional observations on emerging American tendencies, prepared especially for the Winona Lake audience. I am highly pleased that the reproduction of these essays by Moody Press serves to focus the attention of American evangelicals upon the frontiers of contemporary theological concern, even as the appearance of most of the material in *Faith and Thought* will hopefully promote the continuing inter- action of British evangelicals with the pressing problems of Protestant thought in our time.

CARL F. H. HENRY
Editor, *Christianity Today*

1

The Decline of the Bultmann Era

AFTER RULING German theology for more than a decade, Rudolf Bultmann is no longer its king. Former students have usurped his throne and are scrambling for the spoils of conquest. While their loose-knit coalition of post-Bultmannian views tends as a whole to fragment Bultmann's presuppositions, their own impact is blunted by internal disagreement.

In other quarters anti-Bultmannian forces are challenging existentialist theology with increasing vigor. European critics heading this anti-Bultmannian offensive include the traditionally conservative school, the *Heilsgeschichte* (salvation-history) movement, and the emerging "Pannenberg school."

THIRD TIME IN A CENTURY

For the third time in our century Continental Protestantism has tumbled into a morass of theological confusion and transition. Apprehension shadows almost all phases of current theological inquiry and reflection; what the final direction of the dogmatic drift will be is now wholly uncertain.

Contemporary European theology underwent its first major reconstruction when Karl Barth projected his crisis-theology in vigorous protest against classic post-Hegelian modernism. As a result, German theologians by the early 1930s were conceding the death of rationalistic liberalism, which Barth had repudiated as "heresy,"

9

and admitting the triumph of dialectical theology[1] over immanental philosophy.[2] Barth's *Kirchenkampf* role against Nazi Socialism, centering in his appeal to a transcendent "Word of God," removed any doubt that theological leadership had fallen his way and gave him almost the status of a Protestant church father. Barthian theology accordingly remained the dominant force in European dogmatics until mid-century.

It was the appearance of the theological essays titled *Kerygma und Mythos* (Hans-Werner Bartsch, editor) that soon eroded the vast influence of Barth's dogmatics. Published in 1948, this symposium included and made prominent Bultmann's essay on "New Testament and Mythology," a work which had but little recognition at its first appearance in 1941.

Barth's early agreement with existentialism[3] had been evident both from his broad dialectical refusal to ground Christian faith in the realm of objective history and knowledge and in the explicitly existential emphasis of his *Römerbrief* (1919). Bultmann conformed this existentialist commitment to several ruling ideas, namely, that *Formgeschichte* (the form-critical evaluation of New Testament sources) establishes what the primi-

---

[1] A type of recent modern theology inspired by Sören Kierkegaard and popularized by Karl Barth and Emil Brunner. It espouses radical divine transcendence; the content of revelation, it is said, cannot be rationally captured in human concepts and propositions, but can only be witnessed to in a counter-balancing yes and no.

[2] An explanation of reality that views nature and man as aspects of God and denies divine transcendence. In its post-Hegelian form this speculation widely influenced Protestantism in the late nineteenth and early twentieth centuries.

[3] A type of philosophy that emphasizes the importance of individual existence in terms of will or decision (rather than reason), over against both scientific and metaphysical views that minimize individuality. In common with dialectical theology, it denies that reality can be known as a rational system. Its main modern sources are Kierkegaard and Heidegger, the former theistic and the latter atheistic in emphasis.

tive Church (rather than what Jesus) taught; that Christian faith requires no historical foundation beyond the mere "thatness" of Jesus' existence; and finally that Christian relevance and acceptance in the modern scientific age require reinterpretation of the New Testament in terms of an existential nonmiraculous prephilosophy. In view of this "creeping naturalism," Barth and Bultmann parted company between 1927 and 1929. In the 1932 revision of his *Kirchliche Dogmatik* Barth openly repudiated existential philosophy, and he has continually added "objectifying" elements in order to protect his dialectical theology against existentialist takeover.

At the same time, by dismissing modern scientific theory as irrelevant to Christian faith and relegating historical criticism to a role of secondary importance, Barth neglected pressing controversies in related fields of exegesis. Bultmann, on the other hand, assigned larger scope both to a naturalistic philosophy of science and to negative historical criticism, and demanded that the New Testament be "demythologized" of its miraculous content. The theology of divine confrontation, he contended, can and must dispense with such proofs and props. The young intellectuals became increasingly persuaded that Barth's "theology of the Word of God" applied the basic dialectical principle less consistently than did Bultmann's reconstruction. In fact, so extensive was their swing to Bultmannism on the seminary campuses that both Barth and Brunner had to concede that "Bultmann is king."[4]

THE STARS ARE FALLING

The wide split in the Bultmann camp has now created a new strategic situation. The differences among the

---

[4]Cf. "Has Winter Come Again? Theological Transition in Europe," *Christianity Today*, Nov. 21, 1960, pp. 3ff.

disciples of Bultmann signal an impending breakup of the total Bultmannian empire. Self-professed "followers" of Bultmann now range from those who regard interpersonal relations[5] alone as significant for encountering God, to those who emphasize a necessary connection between the historical Jesus and the content of Christian faith. In his retirement, Bultmann has become but a symbolic ruler of the theological kingdom. Meantime an oligarchy of post-Bultmannians—many of them formerly students under Bultmann—has seized the intellectual initiative and is now best known for pointed criticisms of Bultmann and for sharp disagreements within its own ranks.

Says Ernst Fuchs of Marburg, "The vitality is now with Bultmann's disciples who are in revolt, not with Bultmann and those who remain loyal."[6]

And Karl Barth of Basel, commenting on *Time* magazine's statement that Bultmann's Marburg disciples "dominate German theology the way the Russians rule chess," remarks, "That's saying too much." The Bultmann forces, he indicates, "are divided among themselves. And," he adds, "Bultmann has become more or less silent." As Emil Brunner of Zürich puts it, "Bultmann's shaky throne gets more shaky day by day."

Aware that a time of theological transition is again in process in which new views are constantly coming to the fore, scholars contemplate the future of Continental theology with mounting uncertainty.

"One of the tragedies of the theological scene today," remarks the Erlangen New Testament scholar

[5]Man-to-man encounter. This emphasis on revelation apart from the recognition of supernatural and transcendent reality finds certain parallels in the secular "death of God" theology now gaining currency.

[6]Except where published sources are indicated, quotations in these essays were elicited in personal interviews or correspondence, usually the former.

Gerhard Friedrich, "is that the theologians outlive the influence of their own theologies. Barth's star has been sinking, and now Bultmann's is sinking too."

"The realm of systematic theology today suffers from a confusion of the frontiers of thought," adds the Hamburg theologian Wenzel Lohff, because there is not yet "a new binding concept."

And Brunner, whose encounter-theology held the line for a season between Barth and Bultmann, himself contends that "no one theology now on the scene can become the theology of the future. The Germans are monists—they want one leader at a time."

Brunner concedes that for the moment Bultmann and Barth remain the strongest contenders for this leadership. And Heidelberg theologian Edmund Schlink believes that "in the field of systematic theology Barth still has more control, while in the New Testament field, it is Bultmann who holds more influence, although his positions are increasingly disputed and disowned."

"Barth has the vitality and he has disciples," notes Fuchs, "whereas Bultmann has the *a prioris* and his disciples have the vitality—that is what distinguishes Bultmann's situation from Barth's. The real trouble is between Bultmann and his disciples."

Commenting not simply on the vitality of the post-Bultmannians but also on the rivalry between them at the very moment when basic Bultmannian positions are under heavy fire, Schlink notes further: "The countercriticism is growing, and the waves of demythology are diminishing."

THE IRRECONCILABLE DIVISIONS

In the eyes of Bultmann's successor in New Testament at Marburg (since 1952), the Bultmannian school has "broken to pieces" during the past ten years. Long a foe of Bultmannism in its German seat of origin, Werner Georg Kümmel has served as president of Europe's Society of New Testament Studies. As he sees the situation, Bultmannism is now irreconcilably split, and New Testament scholarship is divided into at least four competing camps:

1. The conservatives, including Otto Michel of Tübingen, Joachim Jeremias of Göttingen, Gustav Stählin of Mainz, Karl Heinrich Rengstorf of Münster, Leonhard Goppelt of Hamburg, and Gerhard Friedrich of Erlangen.[7]

2. The *Heilsgeschichte* scholars, a mediating group to which Oscar Cullmann of Basel provides a kind of transition from the first category. Kümmel lists himself here, as well as Eduard Schweizer of Zürich, Eduard Lohse of Berlin, and Ulrich Wilckens of Berlin.

3. The post-Bultmannian scholars.

4. The so-called Pannenberg scholars. Led by Mainz theologian Wolfhardt Pannenberg, this school stresses the reality of objective divine revelation in history and the universal validity of the Christian truth-claim.

5. Independents whose viewpoints defy group identification. Helmut Thielicke of Hamburg, for example, combines liberal, dialectical, and conservative theological ingredients. Cullmann may be listed here also; he so modifies traditional views that he prefers not to be identified as a conservative. On the other hand, many *Heilsgeschichte* scholars brush aside his positions as too conservative. Ethelbert Stauffer of Erlangen is widely associated with a revival of radical liberalism in conservative garb.

---

[7]On the Continent even the most conservative New Testament scholars tend to make concessions to biblical criticism not characteristic of American fundamentalism. No faculty member of the university-related seminaries champions an inerrant Scripture. Some independent institutions support this view, however.

REVOLT IN THE CAMP

Kümmel traces the death knell of the Bultmannian school to Ernst Käsemann's "revolutionary" paper of 1954 on the historical Jesus (*"Das Problem des historischen Jesus"*): "We cannot deny the identity of the exalted Lord with the incarnate Lord without falling into Docetism, and depriving ourselves of the possibility of distinguishing the Church's Easter faith from a myth." Since that time interest in the "happenedness" of something more than the mere existence of Jesus has advanced until most of Bultmann's disciples have come to insist for both theological and historical reasons that some knowledge of the historical Jesus is indispensable. As a result, dialogue was inevitable with such New Testament scholars as Cullmann, Michel, Jeremias, Kümmel, Goppelt, and Stauffer, who had never been uninterested in the historical Jesus and who opposed Bultmann's theology for a variety of other reasons as well.

Not only Bultmann but also Barth deplored this revival of interest in the historical Jesus. In his report, "How My Mind Has Changed," Barth voiced strong suspicions of "the authoritative New Testament men, who to my amazement have armed themselves with swords and staves, and once again undertaken the search for the 'historical Jesus'—a search in which I now as before prefer not to participate."[8]

Nonetheless the historical Jesus became an increasing concern of Bultmann's former students—including Fuchs of Marburg, Ebeling of Zürich, Bornkamm of Heidelberg, if not of almost the entire Bultmannian school. Only a minority resisted this historical interest—former Bultmann students like Hans Conzelmann of

[8]"Recapitulation Number Three," second in a series "How My Mind Has Changed," *The Christian Century,* Jan. 20, 1960, p. 75.

Göttingen, Philipp Vielhauer of Bonn, Manfred Mezger of Mainz, and, on the American side, James M. Robinson of Claremont.

Bultmann himself helped to create the popular distinction between "genuine" and "spurious" disciples of Bultmannism by commending the theological consequences of Herbert Braun's views. Together with Mezger, his faculty colleague, Braun stresses interpersonal relationships alone as decisive for divine revelation. Although both "genuine" and "spurious" groups retain Bultmann's emphasis that the task of exegesis is existential interpretation, the genuine disciples renounce a basic interest in the historical Jesus, while the spurious promote this interest.

Käsemann of Tübingen is the most disaffected member of the Bultmann school; in fact, some observers put him in a class by himself. He speaks of his former teacher as "a man of the nineteenth century" and tells classes that when the Marburg scholar substitutes existential interpretation for New Testament tradition he is simply "looking at his own navel." With an eye on Bultmann's "Eschatology and History," he charges that Bultmann's theology is no longer Christian. Käsemann repudiates Bultmann's anthropological emphasis. He denies also the existential exegesis which Fuchs and Ebeling retain alongside their stress on the importance of the historical Jesus for faith. Although Käsemann sees no sure way to go behind the Gospels to the historical Jesus, he recognizes the difficulty of the form-critical method, namely, that it cannot tell either where Jesus speaks or where the Church speaks. He resumes some of the basic emphases of conservative New Testament scholars—for example, the Jewish rather than Hellenic background of the New Testament ("all Torah must be fulfilled")—and shows interest in New Testament apocalyptic. For Käsemann what is central for primitive Christian preaching is not the believing subject (as with Bultmann) but the interpretation of the eschatological teaching with its anticipation of final fulfillment: God sent his Son, and this has apocalyptic significance. The *Jesusbild,* or picture of Jesus, of Matthew's Gospel is *eo ipso* the historical Jesus. It is equally significant that the problem of *Heilsgeschichte*—of the meaning of certain acts of God for proclamation—again comes into the foreground. In his deviation from Bultmann's methodology at the point of emphasis on the New Testament as the proclamation of an apocalyptic happening, Käsemann occupies a position between most of the post-Bultmannian scholars and the non-Bultmannian "history of salvation" scholars. It is this exegetical turn which accounts for the fact that in New Testament discussion today the most lively theological encounter is occurring between the "moderately" critical *Heilsgeschichte* scholars and the energetic critics of Bultmann in his own camp.

Except for a very small colony of "genuine" Bultmannians, most of Bultmann's former students and disciples now modify or reject his emphasis that "the *preached* Jesus" is the ground of community between God and men. Fuchs and Ebeling seek to correlate the philosophical side of Bultmann's position with some of Luther's motifs as a corrective. Their conviction that the basis of community between God and men is the *historical* Jesus means, further, that the historical Jesus is the One who must be preached. "The historical Jesus —not the preached Jesus—is the one theme of the New Testament," insists Fuchs. Bultmann's failure to say this, he adds, is "the cause of the trouble among his disciples, and is a serious error."

THE MAINZ RADICALS

Eyeing the elements of ambiguity in Bultmann's presentation, Fuchs observes: "Where Bultmann stands sometimes only God knows and not even Bultmann." Confusion over Bultmann's position grew apace when he approved the consequences of the theology of Herbert Braun and Manfred Mezger, the so-called ".Mainz radicals," who stay with "the kerygmatic Christ" and do not revive the quest for the historical Jesus.[9]

These Mainz theologians (Mezger is a former student of Bultmann; Braun, a friend) consider themselves—rightly or wrongly—the heirs of the dialectical theology, and carry Bultmann's position to greater extremes than do other Bultmannian disciples. They question the possibility of speaking of God as a being independent and distinguishable from the world and man. From the Incarnation Mezger concludes that God is not an exceptional reality but a totally profane reality, and that all facts and acts of faith must be encountered in our world in personal relationships. Mezger defines God as the *Unobjectifiable* and *Unutilizable* who encounters us always and only through our neighbor. Revelation for Mezger is the Word that meets me unconditionally, so that I can only trust or reject. Braun, too, insists that revelation shows itself "only where and when I am struck by it."

But despite his approving references to the results of Braun's theology,[10] Bultmann considers some formulations of his Mainz disciples as objectionable and dangerous insofar as they leave in doubt the reality of God.

---

[9]See *"Das Verhaltnis der urchristlichen Christusbotschaft zum historischen Jesus,"* a lecture at Heidelberg Academy of Sciences in which Bultmann replied to scholars reviving the quest for the historical Jesus. The English translation appears in *The Historical Jesus and the Kerygmatic Christ,* Carl L. Braaten and Roy A. Harrisville, eds. (New York: Abingdon Press, 1964). Note Bultmann's remark: "It may be that Herbert Braun's intention to give an existential interpretation has been carried out most consistently" (pp. 35 ff.).

[10]Most recently in *"Der Gottesgedanke und der modern Mensch,"* *Zeitschrift fur Theologie und Kirche,* Dec. 1963, pp. 335-48, reprint of an article which appeared first in the daily newspaper *Die Welt* under the title *"Ist Gott Tod?"*

Bultmann distinguishes reality and objectivity; he denies that God is knowable objectively, insists that revelation occurs only in decision and that God always confronts us when there is revelation. "If Mezger and Braun depict revelation as occurring in personal relationships and dispense with the reality as well as with the objectivity of God, they are in error," he says. "I will not dissolve the faith in revelation into subjectivism. The danger of Braun's formulations is that he seems to do so, although I do not believe he intends this."

The irony of this situation is that Bultmann's criticism of the "Mainz radicals" is not dissimilar from Emil Brunner's criticism of some of Bultmann's own recent formulations. "The concept of revelation has been a dispensable luxury in Bultmann's scheme," Brunner remarks, pointing to Bultmann's delineation of God as the transcendent in the immanent, the unconditional in the conditional. Brunner quotes him: "Only the idea of God which seeks and finds the unconditioned in the conditioned, the other-worldly in the this-worldly, the transcendent in the present reality, is acceptable to modern man."[11] "Bultmann is a modern Origen," says Brunner, "an allegorist of the Alexandrine school. Bultmann has always been a student of Heidegger, who transforms the New Testament for him. Heidegger is an avowed atheist; he bows to no revelation—understands none, needs none, allows none. He smiles at Bultmann for 'making theology out of my philosophy.' "

BULTMANN AND HIS DISCIPLES

Rudolf Bultmann singles out Hans Conzelmann of Göttingen and Erich Dinkler of Heidelberg as his most representative disciples whose results stand closest to

---

[11]*Ibid.,* pp. 346 ff.

his own and whose theology consistently veers away from the relevance of the historical Jesus. When pressed for additional names of "genuine disciples" Bultmann lists almost all of his former students, despite their deviations. "Although I cannot say with certainty, I think they all go along," he remarked, "though with many modifications." In such generalities, Bultmann reveals his awareness that, while none of his former students (Mezger, Conzelmann, Dinkler, Fuchs, Ebeling, Schweizer, Bornkamm, Vielhauer, Käsemann, Kümmel) breaks in all respects with basic Bultmannian positions, yet their departures therefrom cannot be minimized nor can the differences among the men themselves.

The significance of the historical Jesus for Christian faith is the controversial issue that divides these scholars.

Not only against the Mainz radicals who emphasize personal relationships exclusively, but also against Bultmann and many post-Bultmannians, Fuchs contends that "community between men is possible only in the community between God and men" and that "the historical Jesus stands in the midst of revelation." Fuchs turns these principles against Braun and Mezger and whoever else seeks to invert them on Bultmann's premises, as well as against post-Bultmannians who are interested in the historical Jesus as he and Ebeling also are, but who are "unsure whether God's presence is dependent on revelation or revelation dependent on God's presence." Both Conzelmann and Käsemann, complains Fuchs, are unclear about how the historical Jesus and revelation are to be correlated. Conzelmann, unlike Käsemann, concedes to radical historical criticism a role even more important than that of existential interpretation, while he nonetheless seeks to be an orthodox Lutheran. And while Bornkamm shares an interest in the historical Jesus, he subscribes also to Bultmann's notion that "the faith came with Easter," while Fuchs, on the other hand, insists that "the faith came from Jesus." Yet when Schweizer of Zürich carries his post-Bultmannian interest in the historical Jesus to the point of inquiry into Jesus' Messianic self-consciousness, Fuchs calls this an illicit undertaking: "The New Testament is dogmatics, and this cannot be translated into historical data."

Bultmann himself meanwhile decries the fact that the growing interest in the historical Jesus may revive an appeal to historical factors in support and proof of faith. He still maintains that history can never provide a fundamental basis for faith and that faith does not need historical legitimation or historical supports. For Bultmann, the kerygma (the primitive Christian proclamation) alone is basic for faith.

Not even a post-Bultmannian like Bornkamm disputes this point of view, despite his insistence that Jesus' pre-Easter preaching contains inner connections with the post-Easter kerygma, and that faith is interested in the content of Jesus' preaching. "Bultmann is completely right," he insists, "in his view that faith cannot be proved, and that the resurrection of Christ is the point of departure."

In conversation Bultmann now seems to move even beyond his earlier limitation of historical interest to Jesus as merely a Jewish prophet and to his death. "We can know that he lived and preached and interpreted the Old Testament; that he deplored Jewish legalism, abandoned ritual purifications, and breached the Sabbath commandment; that he was not an ascetic, and was a friend of harlots and sinners; that he showed sympathy to women and children, and performed exorcisms." In fact, in Wiesbaden, where Bultmann was seeking cure of an ailment, he was almost disposed to allow that Jesus healed the sick!

Nevertheless, Bultmann's theological outlook can tolerate no return to the historical Jesus as decisive for faith. His readiness to minimize the clash between his disciples must be understood in this context. "We agree that the historical Jesus is the origin of Christianity and agree in the paradox that an historical person is also the eschatological fact which is always present in the Word." By insisting on the event of Jesus Christ, Bultmann aims to distinguish the kerygmatic Christ from any mere Gnostic redeemer-myth.

Now it is true that Bultmann is formally right in insisting that the Easter message is the decisive starting point of Christian faith. He wants no return to the historical Jesus that would erase a decisive break between the historical Jesus and "the Easter event." But his repudiation of the Easter fact, his "demiracleizing" of the Gospels, and his abandonment of the question of the historical Jesus as a theologically fundamental question all rob this emphasis of power. The complaint has widened that his complete rejection of any theological significance for Jesus of Nazareth does violence to apostolic Christianity. Bultmann's view seemed more and more—his intention to the contrary—to dissolve apostolic proclamation into a Christ-myth through his one-sided severance of the kerygma from the event it proclaims and his censorship of the relevance of the historical Jesus.

BREAKDOWN OF BULTMANN'S POSITIONS

While the broken defense of existentialist positions has thus divided the Bultmannian camp, the assault from outside has increased in scope and depth. Over against Bultmann not only post-Bultmannians, but also the

Heilsgeschichte scholars and the Pannenberg school as well as traditionally conservative scholars, are demanding the recognition of a Christian starting point also in the life and teaching of the historical Jesus. "The smoke over the frontiers has lifted," reports Leonhard Goppelt of Hamburg, "and a new generation is in view. Bultmann's spell is broken, and the wide range of critical discussion signals an open period. Now that a shift from Bultmann is under way in a new direction, we are on the threshold of a change as significant as that of a century ago, when Hegelian emphases gave way to the neo-Kantianism of Ritschl."

As Joachim Jeremias of Göttingen sees it, the vulnerability of Bultmann's theological structure is evident from the fact that three of its fundamental emphases are now more or less shattered:

1. Bultmann's neglect of the historical Jesus has broken down, and a deliberate return to the historical Jesus now characterizes New Testament studies. In deference to Wellhausen, Bultmann held that Jesus was but a Jewish prophet and that his life and message were not of great importance for Paul. The untenability of this position is now clear, and it is widely agreed that Christianity cannot be truly understood without a return to the historical Jesus.

2. Bultmann placed great weight on an alleged Gnosticism which supposedly influenced the Gospel of John and other New Testament literature. But the Dead Sea Scrolls show that the dualism of John's Gospel is Palestinian and Judaic. A monograph by Carsten Colpe is widely credited with demonstrating convincingly that the model of a pre-Christian Gnostic redeemer-myth which Bultmann locates behind New Testament writings is actually nothing but the myth of Manicheanism of the third century A.D., which very likely sprang from a Docetic Christology repudiated by historic Christianity.

3. Bultmann defined the task of exegesis as the existential understanding of the New Testament, and he therefore stressed anthropology: "The Gospel gives me a new understanding of myself." But "the Gospels stress theology, and they give us new knowledge of God," counters Jeremias, one of the most articulate spokesmen for traditional conservative positions. Jeremias comments that "the history of the Church has shown that it is always dangerous when New Testament exegesis takes its method from contemporary philosophy, whether the idealistic philosophy of the nineteenth century or the existentialist philosophy of the twentieth century."

It remains true nonetheless that Bultmann's followers —whether "genuine" or "spurious"—perpetuate many methodological and critical presuppositions integral to Bultmann's theology. Despite their interest in the historical Jesus, even the deviationist disciples retain Bultmann's notion that the task of exegesis is existential interpretation. But this basic Bultmannian assumption is challenged by Kümmel, a spokesman for the *Heilsgeschichte* school. Kümmel repudiates the presupposition that the task of exegesis is to discover the self-understanding of the New Testament writers in order to correct our self-understanding. The real task of hermeneutics, he says pointedly, is to find out what the New Testament teaches. The New Testament is "a revelation of the history of salvation," he insists, and he is confident that the critically founded search for the historical Jesus will "win the field." Kümmel emphasizes that "the facts, not the kerygma, evoke my response."

AN UNREPENTANT BULTMANN

Bultmann remains unconvinced that his presuppositions have been shaken. He hardly regards himself as an emperor in exile or about to be deposed. Of his *a prioris*, he considers the second (as Jeremias lists them) less important than the others, but even with respect to the supposed Gnostic background of the New Testament he clings still to the position that the theology of the Fourth Gospel and of Paul is influenced by Gnostic views. In fact, Bultmann is currently writing a commentary on John's Epistles from this perspective to round out his earlier work on John's Gospel. Bultmann attaches more importance, however, to his other *a prioris* regarding the historical Jesus and existential understanding, which, he says, "stand together." Although he professes also to be "interested in" the historical Jesus, he speaks only of Jesus' deeds, and of these in attenuated and nonmiraculous form. Contrary to the nineteenth century "life of Jesus" school, he insists that we know nothing of Jesus' personality, and considers this no real loss. "What does it matter?" he asks. "What counts is his Word and his Cross which is the same now as then." While Bultmann does not destroy continuity between the historical Jesus and the New Testament kerygma, he nonetheless denies continuity between the historical Jesus and the Christ of the kerygma. As he sees it, the kerygma requires only the "that" of the life of Jesus and the fact of his crucifixion. In other words, the kerygma presupposes but mythologizes the historical Jesus.

The issues of central importance, according to Bultmann, are the historical method and *Formgeschichte* in biblical theology, and the problem of history and its interpretation in hermeneutics, the latter being "connected with anthropological and philosophical problems."

The complaint that he virtually abandons the concept of revelation Bultmann attributes to a misunderstanding of his thought and intention. He insists now as always on the reality of revelation, but he distinguishes *Offenbarheit* from *Offenbarung*—that is, revelation as an objectifiable fact from revelation as an act. In Bultmann's sense, "genuine revelation" is always only an act, never an objectified fact. "Revelation happens only in the moment when the Word of God encounters me."

But for all Bultmann's self-assurance, European theology is increasingly moving outside the orbit of his control and influence. The so-called "Bultmann school" has never really been a unit, even if his disciples all work within similar critical and methodological assumptions. While they build on Bultmann as the most important New Testament theologian of our time, they now separate the two emphases which Bultmann conjoined: radical criticism of the trustworthiness of the Gospels and existential interpretation. Heidegger's dark and harsh image of man, which so neatly fit the mood of a postwar generation plagued by anxiety, became most important for Bultmann's disciples. The Fuchs-Ebeling line of existential exegesis turned Bultmann's New Testament ideas into dogmatics à la Heidegger. But Bultmann's disciples have increasingly pulled back from his views or moved around them in some respects, each man emphasizing a perspective which diverges from Bultmann—sometimes dealing severely with him —and combating other post-Bultmannians as well. More and more, Bultmann's followers distinguish his exegetical and historical work from his philosophical and dogmatic intention. But none of the post-Bultmannians has so united the relevant data from a new perspective as to be able to shape a coherent alternative to Bultmann's view.

Attacks on Bultmann's position from outside his camp have become sharper and sharper and have exploited the interior divisions. Heinrich Schier, a former

Bultmann student and disciple, became a Roman Catholic and is now teaching in Bonn. "Bultmann is a rationalist and neo-Ritschlian," says Emil Brunner. "He seeks to overcome nihilism, which endangers his position, but his alternative is never quite clear." And Peter Brunner, the Heidelberg theologian, points a finger at Bultmann's "weakest point": "In *Glauben und Verstehen* he nowhere tells us what a minister must say in order to articulate the Gospel, nor what (besides the name of Jesus and his cross) is the binding or given content of the message to be perpetuated. He presupposes that a message comes to the individual, and discusses the problem of the individual to whom the message comes, and how it is to be grasped. But if one raises the question of proclamation into the future, it becomes clear that Bultmann has not resolved the problem of content." Says Otto Weber, the Göttingen theologian: "In a word, the reason for the breakdown of Bultmann's theology is his existentialism." And from Basel Karl Barth's verdict has echoed throughout Europe: "Thank God, Bultmann doesn't draw the consistent consequences and demythologize God!"

Criticism of Bultmann's theology is increasing. Many scholars observe that while Bultmann scorns all philosophy as culture-bound and transitory, he nonetheless exempts existentialism. In his existential "third heaven" he claims to have exclusive leverage against the whole field of thought and life. But existentialism is no heaven-born absolute; it is very much a modern philosophical scheme. Any translation of New Testament concepts into existential categories must result in a version no less "limited"—linguistically and historically—than the biblical theology the existentialists aim to "purify." The Bultmannians assume, moreover, that the New Testament writers, since they were especially interested in their subject, must have transformed (and deformed) the historical facts of the Gospels. This premise the existentialists fail to apply to their own special interest in the kerygma. While the Bultmannians rid themselves of the miracle of objective revelation, they seem to endow their subjectivity with a secret objectivity, and abandon the apostolic miracles only to make room for their own.

SIGNS OF A BULTMANN-TILLICH MERGER

The theological scene now reflects increasing prospect of a synthesis of the viewpoints of Bultmann and Tillich. Talk of such a synthesis signifies that neither man's position has fully won a permanent hold, and that disciples of both are seeking exterior reinforcement. Otto Weber of Göttingen has recently noted the growing impact of Tillich's philosophy upon Bultmann's position, because Tillich's thought includes an appealing apologetic element absent from Bultmann's presentation.

Quite understandably, Bultmann would be less than happy over a synthesis. All such mergers of systems are ideological reductions, and they imply that neither of the positions involved is independently adequate. Bultmann still criticizes Tillich's view as "less Christological and more philosophical"; one critic notes that Bultmann promotes independence of all philosophy, *existentialism excepted*. Moreover, Bultmann disowns Tillich's interest in psychology and depth psychology, because of his own distinction of true-being and non-being and his understanding of man on the basis of *Worthaftigkeit*.[12]

---

[12]The German term is as unusual as the English translation "wordliness" used by the translator of Gerhard Ebeling's *Word and Faith*. Its apparent intention is to emphasize that reality and revelation are inseparable (haften, "bind") from word.

Nonetheless, some components are common to both viewpoints, and there are noteworthy similarities between the two scholars. Both have influenced many young intellectuals—divinity students more than scientists. Both are more theological in their sermons than in their systematic theology. Both oppose traditional dogmatics and ontology from the standpoint of critical reason. Both reject any knowledge of God objective to personal decision. In respect to anthropology, moreover, Bultmann says Tillich and he concur. Both scholars have sharply accommodated Christianity to modern philosophy of science. Yet Bultmann professedly seeks a Christological systematics, while Tillich's structure is more obviously that of a religious philosophy.

Bultmann insists on the reality of a personal God who specially confronts all men in the Word alone; Tillich, on the other hand, considers personality as applied to the Unconditioned purely symbolic, and finds a special side in all general revelation. Tillich's influence in Europe has thus far been impeded by his lack of emphasis on historical criticism and on the newer exegesis ruling the field. Aspects of his thought, however, are now being reworked by the so-called Pannenberg scholars, who consider history and exegesis within the framework of a revelational concept. Above all else, the trend toward a synthesis of these systems signifies that both European and American liberalism have entered upon a major period of dissatisfaction and transition.

2

The Deterioration of Barth's Defenses

AMONG THE MANY ISSUES raised by contemporary theology, one question is persistent:

Why was the theology of Karl Barth unable to stem the tide of Rudolf Bultmann's theories?

No Continental theologian is disposed to conduct a postmortem examination of Barth's theology; to do so would be to suggest that its influence were something wholly past. But this is not the case. Emil Brunner regards Barth as Bultmann's greatest present contender, and many others concur that both the Basel theologian and his theology are still "very much alive." In French-speaking Switzerland Barthian theology has always held greater sway than Bultmannian theories. And on the German scene, Heidelberg theologian Edmund Schlink thinks Barth's influence is not only far from spent but actually expanding in some quarters.

Nor are European theologians ready to minimize the differences between Barth and Bultmann, differences which have increased markedly with the years. Often, in fact, the divergences are even exaggerated—for example, by assigning more weight than Barth allows to the "objectifying" elements in his theology, or by imputing to Bultmann a denial of the reality of God in view of his stress on subjectivity. Such distortions aside, the contrariety of their positions cannot be denied. "A wide gulf," says Erlangen theologian Wilfried D. Joest, "separates the emphasis that God has *no objective reality* at all, but exists only for me, from the emphasis that concedes that there is *no objective revelation,* yet as-

30

serts an objective reality that cannot be objectified by methods of reason and must be won by faith."

BARTH AND BULTMANN

As the Bultmann school reiterated its belief in the *reality* of God, however, and stressed the necessity of a consistently dialectical theology against Barth's exposition, this "wide gulf" seemed to disappear. Even the "Mainz radicals" speak of Barth and Bultmann as representing complementary rather than opposing viewpoints. "It is not a matter of either/or between Barth and Bultmann," says Manfred Mezger, "for each theology needs the other as a corrective." Why so? we might ask. "So Barth does not forget the *anthropological* relevance of theology," continues Mezger, "and so Bultmann does not forget the genuine root (revelation) of theology. Barth's basic principle (the absoluteness or divinity of God) has as its logical consequence that *no* advance reservations are possible for revelation." Once this is said, the Mainz school is poised to feed the lamb to the lion in the interest of a Bultmannized Barth: "We emphasize that man does not need to recognize God *first* and then recognize reality, but the recognition of reality is coincidental with the recognition of the reality of God. Barth says, 'first the dicta about God, and then the statements about man'; Bultmann says, 'every dictum about God has to be said simultaneously about man.' Barth's principal thesis 'God is God' is useless nonsense. God is not absolute in the metaphysical sense but is absolute only in the *'geschichtliche'* sense of always occurring. We have not seen God and know absolutely nothing about God except what He is saying. *All dicta* of theological origin must and can only be verified anthropologically."

However much Barth may deplore existentialism,

however much he may reinforce the "objectifying" factors in his theology and appeal to wider and fuller aspects of the biblical witness, his position has remained vulnerable to Bultmannian counterattack. Bultmann was one of the earliest sympathizers with the Barthian revolt against objective historical method, a revolt that Bultmann then carried to a non-Barthian climax by imparting an existential turn to the distinction between the *historisch* as mere objective past occurrence and the *geschichtlich* as revelatory present encounter.[1] In the revision of his *Church Dogmatics,* Barth had sought to divorce dialectical from existential theology; this effort Bultmann fought vigorously. On the premise that Barth expounds the dialectical view uncertainly whereas Bultmann does so comprehensively, the Bultmannian scholars turned the main tide of student conviction away from Barth and toward Bultmann.

"The great effect of Barth's theology," remarks Bultmann, "was that it destroyed subjectivism. Barth said God is not a symbol of my own religiosity, but He confronts me. In this we agree. And we agree also in the dialectical method insofar as Barth says theological propositions are genuine only if they are not universal truths. But Barth applies the dialectical method inconsistently: many of his propositions are 'objectivizing' propositions—and this I have sought to eliminate in my own theology."

Walter Kreck, Reformed theologian at Bonn, and

[1]The basic distinction between history as act (*Geschichte*) and history as record (*Historie*) is exemplified by the Bible, which also refers to divine acts (divine fore-ordination) that cannot be objects of historical research. In contemporary theology, this distinction has been further applied to divine acts within history. Since the divine or miraculous element in events (e.g., the resurrection in distinction from the empty tomb) cannot be described in terms of scientific history, some theologians have pressed the distinction into two kinds of events (*Geschichte*) implying both a denial of the this-worldly aspects of God's actions, and an acceptance of the view that historians may legitimately ignore them.

one of Barth's former students who still regards himself
as broadly a Barth disciple, concedes that the differences between Barth and Bultmann have receded
further into the background. "Both Barth and Bultmann reject objective revelation. Barth and Bultmann
have dialectical theology in common, and their main
difference lies in Barth's methodological rejection of
existential interpretation. Bultmann fears that Barth's
method leads to a false objectivity, and insists that his
existential exegesis alone prevents this. Barth fears Bultmann's method leads to a false subjectivity, and insists
that his emphasis alone preserves the reality of revelation. Yet, for all their differences," Kreck concludes,
"to many scholars the two positions no longer look as
far apart as they once did."

AN INNER CONNECTION?

Is there an inherent relationship, a principial continuity, between Barth's theology and Bultmann's? Or is
there rather a vacuum in Barth's thought that made
his dogmatics vulnerable to Bultmannian counterattack? Why did Barthian theology, which held sway in
Germany for half a generation, lose its hold in the face
of Bultmannian existentialism? These questions press
for an answer. Aside from circumstantial factors—for
example, Schlink's indication of political considerations
(Barth's influence in Germany was retarded by his
failure to oppose Communism as strenuously as he did
National Socialism)—what accounts theologically for
the fact that Barthianism, which had routed post-Hegelian rationalistic modernism, could not stem the surge
toward Bultmann's revival of the old modernism in
connection with *existenz?*[2]

Heidelberg theologians suggest two critical areas of

[2] A technical term used in modern German philosophy to
locate each individual person's uniqueness and freedom in
human decision, in contrast with efforts to define man's significance in terms of a rational system.

weakness. Schlink, for instance, doubts that an inherent principial connection exists between Barth's and Bultmann's formulations. Barth, says Schlink, was "more systematic than historical, and he did not deal adequately with the historical aspects of Christian faith. After the Second World War, many problems were again raised at this level, and it was apparent that Barth's exposition had not really met them." Schlink's associate, Peter Brunner, singles out "the historical facet" also as one of the weaknesses in Barth's theology which Bultmannians were able to exploit. As Brunner sees it, Barth treated too naïvely the question of what historical reasoning can tell us about the facts in which God has revealed himself; indeed, Barth totally suppressed these facts from a purely historical view. Bultmann, on the other hand, took his negative approach seriously, and sought to destroy every effort to find revelation by historical investigation.

Besides Barth's indifference to the historical, exploited by Bultmann, Brunner adduces "the decision facet" as a second major Barthian weakness. For Barth there is no saving moment in time (the saving moment is an eternal moment). But, observes Peter Brunner, theology must not overlook the importance of this time-event in which man here-and-now encounters the Word of the Cross. Contrary to Barth, Bultmann stresses the event of encounter with the Word here-and-now. For Barth, the salvation of every man is settled in the eternal election of the man Jesus, and the means of grace are significant only for the cognition of salvation, not for the transmission of salvation. Barth and Bultmann agree this far: that without the Living Word of God here-and-now, which is the Word of God for me, one cannot experience the reality of revelation. But when Barth detached the transmission of salvation from the means of grace he opened the door, as Peter Brunner sees it, for Bultmann's wholly existential setting.

Does this mean that the history of twentieth-century theology will reduce Barth and Bultmann to one theological line? The Heidelberg theologians think not.

Some theologians are less reluctant than the Heidelberg theologians to identify an inner principial connection in the Barth-Bultmann formulations. They insist rather that the transition of influence from Barth to Bultmann was inevitable because of presuppositions common to both systems, presuppositions to which Bultmann allowed greater impact than did Barth. "Theologians of a later century," says Erlangen theologian Wilfried D. Joest, "will look back and see one line from Barth to Bultmann, and in this movement they will recognize the same type of theology, despite deep-rooted differences."

Actually, such assessments are not only a future expectation. Theologians both to Barth's right and to his left are already insisting that certain *a prioris* common to Barth and Bultmann explain the sudden fall of Barth's theological leadership, and, in fact, the present predicament of Continental theology. Graduate students in European seminaries increasingly view Bultmann's position as "an automatic development from Barth's"; and in the few remaining Bultmann centers they picture the dialectical Barth rather than the demythologizing Bultmann as the "fairy tale dogmatician."

The essential connection between the two theologians is the basic emphasis that God meets us personally in the Word and makes this Word his own. With this relationship in view, Otto Michel, the New Testament scholar at Tübingen, asserts that "Barth and Bultmann are two parts of one and the same movement of dialectical theology. Barth begins with the Word of God and defines this in relation to human *existenz*. Bultmann inverts this; he begins with man's *existenz* and relates this to kerygma." "Neither Barth nor Brunner," says Michel, "gave earnest weight to historical questions —the origin of certain of the biblical elements and theological content, and their relevance for dogmatic questions. The objectivity in Barth's theology is not an object of historical research. Only by way of philosophical construction does Barth avoid subjectivizing revelation."

Adolf Köberle, the Tübingen theologian, singles out the Barthian discontinuity between revelation and history as a decisive central point of contact with Bultmann's delineation. Barth's "prophetic" role, says Köberle, involved him in a broad and bold criticism of modernism in which he too hurriedly brushed aside some of the fundamental and crucial problems of contemporary theology. Regarding this broad prophetic proclamation, Köberle thinks it not impossible that Barth may exercise in dogmatics somewhat the same influence as Billy Graham in evangelism. Barth "failed fully to engage the historical background of the New Testament, and this failure gave competing scholars an opportunity to correlate the data with contrary conclusions." Köberle points to Barth's neglect of such questions as the relationship of Christianity and science and of revelation and history, and his indifference to the problem of supposed Hellenistic or late Jewish apocalyptic influence in the New Testament.

Wolfgang Trillhaas, teacher of systematic theology at Göttingen, and former student there of Barth, has broken with his mentor's dogmatics, because "Barth so oriented his theology to critical questions and to critical reason that Bultmann could snatch away the initiative."

Trillhaas recognizes the differing intentions of the two theologians, and is aware of Barth's efforts to guard his systematics against subjectivizing miscarriages of it. Says Trillhaas, "Both Barth and Bultmann had an interest in the speciality of Christian revelation. But through philosophical speculation Bultmann gave this interest a radically destructive interpretation, whereas Barth has sought increasingly to purge himself from the earlier philosophical influences." Trillhaas considers Barth's scheme still vulnerable, however, particularly in its severance of revelation from reason.

BARTH AND BRUNNER

Among the theologians at Erlangen and Hamburg, Emil Brunner's influence is greater than Barth's. Nonetheless it is Barth more than Brunner who penetrates the mainstream of dialectical controversy. Brunner's illness has hampered his creative and productive effort and removed him from theological engagement; in the aftermath of his stroke he spends much time indoors. Brunner has become more mellow over his differences with Barth, and with a twinkle he comments to visiting students: "I'm a Barthian. I always have been." But he nonetheless considers certain facets of Barth's system unnecessarily weak. Among his favorite anecdotes is that of the lady theologian who embraced him warmly and said: "Barth saved me from liberalism, and you saved me from Barth."

The strength of Brunner's theology has always rested in its recognition of general revelation. Its weakness, along with Barth's, centers in the dialectical presuppositions that relate revelation only tenuously with history and reason. In his revision of *Truth as Encounter,* which now appears under the title *Theology Beyond Barth and Bultmann* (Westminster Press, 1964), Brunner stresses that Christianity must be more than merely negative toward philosophy. While he calls for a Christian philosophy, he does not modify his dialectical approach to revelation and reason. His philosophical treatment of the idea of truth as encounter still excludes revealed propositions and a revealed world-life view.

Brunner's theology also lost ground as he strengthened its basic personalistic philosophy. This reinforcement gave his thought an individualistic touch that—so Wenzel Lohff of Hamburg thinks—prevented Brunner "from fully appropriating the dimensions of the newer Christological and ecclesiological thought." Yet because of its clarity, Brunner's work remains useful among lay theologians. Theologian Anders Nygren of Lund notes that Brunner indeed freed the Christian doctrine of God of Platonic and neo-Platonic speculation. In doing so, however, he attached it instead, says Nygren, to "an I-thou philosophy and a kind of philosophical actualism" which represents still another compromise "between a philosophical thinking and the revelation."[3] In any event, Bultmannian theologians exploited Brunner's emphasis on the divine-human encounter for their own contrary objectives, and Brunner's affliction left him a less formidable foe than Barth.

In Europe's present theological turmoil, Brunner anticipates "a little return" to his own theology which "held the line between Barth and Bultmann" for a time. "The best option is my own," he insists. But Brunner seems to underestimate the difficulty of regaining a strategic position on the fast-changing frontier of European thought, particularly when a theology that has served for a season and has lost its hold no longer commands the center of debate.

Pro-Barthian theologians are sobered by the fact that the already bypassed options will hardly enjoy more than a limited revival. Neither Barth nor Bultmann is likely to dominate the European theological situation

[3]See *The Theology of Emil Brunner,* Charles W. Kegley, ed. (New York: The Macmillan Co., 1962), p. 183.

again. Some scholars are now asking if the deterioration of Barthian defenses under Bultmannian assault, and the subsequent collapse of Bultmannian positions, perhaps portend a radical reconstruction of Continental theology.

Barth registered his most comprehensive Christological emphasis immediately after World War II. Barth deduced theological and ethical positions from Christological analogies, and tended to overlook empirical concerns and critical historical investigation. While many scholars felt it necessary, therefore, to go beyond Barth's compromised historical interest, they were forced nevertheless to keep in touch with Barth because of his active participation in the theological controversy. At the age of 79,[4] however, the ailments of declining years turn Barth's thoughts more often to "the tent that is beginning to be dissolved," as he puts it. While he continues his monthly student colloquiums in the upstairs room of Restaurant Bruderholz near his home in Basel, Barth's creative work has begun to lag, and he feels unsure about completing his *Church Dogmatics.*

Busily but cautiously Barth has been modifying his theology in the direction of objectivity in order to escape Bultmannian expropriation. "Barth has become almost a Protestant scholastic again," chuckles Gerhard Friedrich, the Erlangen New Testament scholar. "More and more he leans on the historical rather than the existential." But the feeling is widespread that the revisions in Barth's theology are "too little and too late." The moving frontier of theological debate is shifting beyond the Barth-Bultmann discussion in a manner that brings some of their common *a prioris* under fire. This means that the revisions in Barth's theology have lagged too long to have any direct impact upon mainline Continental theology.

[4]Barth will be 80 on May 10, 1966.

THE NEW FRONTIERS

The formative theology of the foreseeable future is not likely to be Barth's, Brunner's, or Bultmann's, but rather an alternative to all three.

The *Heilsgeschichte* school is calling for a fuller correlation of revelation and history. The traditional conservative scholars have long attacked dialectical theology in even wider dimensions. And a revolt against dialectical theology has been under way among several followers of Wolfhardt Pannenberg of Mainz, a former student of Barth. In his bold insistence on objective historical revelation, Pennenberg represents the farthest contemporary break from Barth and Bultmann and the dialectical theology.

Says Pannenberg: "Barth and Bultmann both insist on the kerygmatical character of the Christian faith and tradition, and both assign the Christian faith (kerygma) independence over against the truth of science and philosophy. Both Barth and Bultmann refuse to bring Christian tradition in relation to the realm of objective knowledge." In spite of his "apparent objectivism," protests Pannenberg, "the later Barth remains a disciple of Herrmann, as is Bultmann." And he adds, "Bultmann is the most faithful exponent of the dialectical theology—more so than Barth."

As Pannenberg sees it, the dialectical theology undermines both historical revelation and the universal validity of Christian truth. He insists that "if one really takes history in earnest, he will find that God has revealed himself *in history*." He maintains the necessity of knowing something about the historical facts on which Christian faith depends. Moreover, he strikes at the dialectical theology's disjunction of revelation and reason, and at its consequent refusal to relate Christianity to the realm of objective knowledge.

3

Basic Issues in Modern Theology: Revelation in History

THE LONG FAILURE of German theology to reject the existential-dialectical notion that the historical aspects of the Christian revelation are dispensable gave to Continental dogmatics something of the atmosphere of an exclusive private club. Membership was restricted mainly to scholars who shared the speculative dogma that spiritual truth cannot be unified with historical and scientific truth. They therefore emphasized the kerygmatic Christ at the expense of the Jesus of history, isolated Christianity from answerability to scientific and historical inquiry, and detached theology from philosophic truth.

Meanwhile British and American theologians and exegetes—whether conservative or liberal and despite sharp differences over the role and outcome of historical criticism—retained a lively interest in historical concerns. Most Anglo-Saxon biblical scholars still repose bold confidence in the historical method. They view the Gospels somewhat as historical source documents, carry forward the research effort to reconstruct the life of Jesus, stress the kerygma's connection with specifically historical factors, and assume generally the concrete historical character of divine revelation.

The current renewal of European interest in biblical history and its bearing on divine revelation encourages many scholars to hope that for the first time theologians and exegetes in America, Britain, and Europe as well may at long last join in theological conversation. Since

British and American scholars currently hold a considerable head start in their commitment to historical concerns, some observers feel that non-European could in fact wrest away the theological initiative long held by the German professors.

Most of today's unrest in Bultmannian circles results from the present sprawling interest in historical questions. Some pro-Bultmannian scholars, of course, still invoke radical historical criticism in support of existentialist exegesis; Conzelmann, for example, insists that the bare fact of Jesus' historical existence is the only datum that can be historically fixed. Even the post-Bultmannian "new quest" for the historical Jesus reflects a continuing loyalty to Ritschl's and Herrmann's subordination of the knowledge of God to faith or trust, so that its historical interest does not lead to evangelical results. But many post-Bultmannians at least share Fuchs' emphasis that "the historical Jesus of the nineteenth century was not really the historical Jesus, but [that] the Jesus of the New Testament, the Jesus of revelation, is." Bultmann's kerygmatic Christology closed the door in principle to any movement behind the kerygma to the historical Jesus. At the same time, he nowhere explains why, on his premises, any continuity whatever is necessary between the *historical cross* and the *preached cross* of the kerygma; nor why, since he insists on this limited continuity, other historical aspects embraced by the kerygma must be excluded.

Yet what sets off post-Bultmannian interest in the historical Jesus from that of the *Heilsgeschichte* scholars is its refusal to regard the historical Jesus as decisive for faith, and also its emphasis that faith requires no historical supports. The salvation-history scholars, by contrast, investigate the revelation-significance of God's acts in history.

Some post-Bultmannians, it is true, take a position at the very edge of *Heilsgeschichte* concerns. Günther Bornkamm, for example, argues that the *Heilsgeschichte* concept cannot be renounced but must be redefined. "Faith must be interested in history," says Bornkamm, "because the name of Jesus in our confession is not a mere word but an historical person." Yet he centers historical interest in the content of Jesus' preaching. He rejects antithesizing history and experience, and stresses that while revelation does not (as he sees it) take place in "history itself," it does occur in the encounter "which belongs to history." Unlike *Heilsgeschichte* scholars, who locate the meaning of history in sacred history, Bornkamm insists that the essence of history is still to be decided. "We are ourselves part of the drama of history and salvation-history. The meaning of history is not given as a *Heilsgeschichte* drama or series of past events of which we are spectators, and to which we need only relate ourselves to accept the divine gift."

Bornkamm complains, moreover, that Ernst Kasemann's view of the relevance of Jewish apocalyptic for Christian faith is contestable. Käsemann, who presses the question of the meaning of certain acts of God for Christian proclamation, stresses over against Bultmann that the real center of primitive Christian proclamation was not the believing subject but rather the interpretation of the eschatological teaching with its anticipation of final fulfillment. The New Testament message, he says, is the proclamation of an apocalyptic event.

HISTORICAL REVELATION

Heilsgeschichte positions differ from post-Bultmannian perspectives in emphasizing that the saving deeds of God supply a ground of faith: Christian faith is faith not only in the kerygmatic Christ but also in the historical Jesus. All *Heilsgeschichte* scholars insist on an integral connection between the saving deeds of God and Christian faith.

Not all members of the salvation-history movement today speak unreservedly of historical revelation, and none would go the distance of the old Erlangen *Heilsgeschichte* school. Their approach sometimes does not transcend an application to New Testament studies of Gerhard von Rad's positions in Old Testament study. Von Rad rejects the old Erlangen view of history as a process whose inner meaning can be demonstrated, and his emphasis on the Old Testament as a collection of confessional traditions of salvation-history leaves the confessional and historical factors unsurely related. He does not regard Jesus' life and work as a direct fulfillment of particular Old Testament prophecies and promises; rather, with the contemporary *Heilsgeschichte* school, he views Jesus as fulfilling the general Old Testament picture only in the broad sense of archetype and type. All *Heilsgeschichte* scholars reject the bare *Religionsgeschichte* view that Jesus incarnates the universal spirit or idea; they look instead in the direction of Von Rad's emphasis that the Old Testament must be interpreted (independently of all developments of nonbiblical religions) as the history of God which was fulfilled in Jesus Christ; and that the New Testament must be interpreted (independently of all religious developments in the old world) as the fulfillment of the Old Testament.

While a mildly conservative New Testament scholar like Goppelt of Hamburg is congenial to these positions, some conservative scholars view the *Heilsgeschichte* wing as little else than a more positive movement of the critical school. The problem is dramatized by the fact that many *Heilsgeschichte* scholars, for all their larger emphasis on biblical history, still hesitate to

regard the meaning of salvation as objectively given
and accessible. Instead, they continue to speak of religious experience or decision as a fulcrum of revelation.
Although he insists that the Old Testament is strictly
a *Heilsgeschichte* process, Goppelt refuses to hold that
divine revelation is given in history, and retains a dialectical perspective despite differences with Bultmann
and Barth. Invoking the Lutheran formula of "in, with,
and under," he asserts that it is too much to say that
the Word is revealed in history.

For the sake of clarity we shall compare the viewpoints of the *Heilsgeschichte* scholars and of the traditional conservative scholars. Both schools agree that
divine revelation and redemption are objective historical realities. They both admit that the sacred
biblical events, like all past happenings, are not accessible to empirical observation, although from written
sources these events are knowable to historians by the
same methods of research used in the study of secular
history.

What, then, of the meaning of the biblical events?
Surely even the immediate observers, whether Pharisees
or apostles, could not have learned this by mere observation. The spiritual meaning of these sacred events
is divinely given, not humanly postulated. Here again
Heilsgeschichte and conservative scholars agree.

But how is this divine meaning of sacred history given
to faith? Conservative scholars insist that the historian
need not shift to some mystical ground or suprarational
existential experience to discern it. For the New Testament documents as they testify to divine deed-revelation
give or *are* themselves divine truth-revelation; that is to
say, the divinely given interpretation of the saving
events is contained within the authoritative record of
the events themselves. Or to put it another way, the
divine saving events include, as a climax, the divine

communication of the meaning of those events, objectively given in the inspired Scriptures. While nobody can infer the meaning of the biblical events from empirical observation or historical inquiry, the doctrines of Christianity are accessible to the historian in the form of the New Testament verbal revelation of God's acts and purposes. Historical investigation deals with the scriptural documents that record the historical disclosure of God's suprahistorical redemptive plan. When conservative scholars assert that God's revelation in history is not found by scientific research but is given to faith, they mean that the Holy Spirit illumines the minds of men to accept the scriptural revelation of the meaning of the events of Christ's life, death, and resurrection. That the truth of apostolic interpretation is grasped only by faith and our acceptance of Scripture is a work of the Holy Spirit is a constant evangelical emphasis.

The *Heilsgeschichte* scholars compromise the conservative view because of their prior critical rejection of the historical Christian understanding of revelation in terms of the infallible divine communication of propositional truths. Their emphasis falls instead upon individual spiritual encounter not only as the focal point of illumination but as the focal point of the revelation of divine meaning. While they insist that revelation is objectively given in historical events, they suspend the knowability of the meaning of that revelation upon subjective decision and isolate it from divine truths and doctrines objectively and authoritatively given in the inspired Scriptures.

A CASE IN POINT

Werner Georg Kümmel of Marburg, a spokesman for the salvation-history school, insists that divine revela-

tion "exists only in response," although his exposition
of this perspective includes many conservative facets.

"Revelation is given not only in history but even in
historical events and the interpretations connected with
these events. Historical critical research is therefore
indispensable for faith that wants to know about the
events and the interpretation connected with them. But
research can find out only the events or the reflex of the
events (e.g., of the resurrection of Christ) and the
claim of the participants to interpret these events in
the way God wants. Whether this claim is correct, research cannot find out, but only faith. So we never *find*
revelation in history by scientific research. But we can
clarify and make clear that their claim and our faith attached to this claim are founded in an event that really
gives the sufficient ground for this faith. So faith does
not depend on historic research but needs it as soon as
faith begins to reflect on itself, for faith does not only
need the certainty of the event-basis but also the good
conscience of not being built in the air."

As Kümmel sees it, by historical research one finds
in Scripture both the sacred events and the meaning
adduced as the kerygma connected with those events.
But, he insists, the unbeliever cannot disallow "the
factuality of the events and the *factuality* of the interpretation given them by the apostolic witnesses,
[whereas] the *validity* of these interpretations is grasped
only by personal response in faith"—in response, moreover, that must be "a *reasoned* response." Apart from
his disjunction of fact from meaning (and not simply
of objective event from subjective appropriation), it
should be clear that Kümmel struggles to elevate the
meaning of saving history above a theology of decision.
Yet he balks at an objectively-given scriptural interpretation which is to be appropriated, as in the conservative tradition, as authoritative propositional informa-

tion. For Kümmel distinguishes proclamation from information and, moreover, subjects the scriptural meaning of salvation-history to possibilities of critical revision. In view of his appeal to "the character of faith as response to a proclamation and not to an information," and of his consequent insistence that the believer "cannot simply repeat what has been said by others, but must try to understand and, perhaps, to reformulate or to criticize the aptness of the apostolic interpretations," one must ask Kümmel what postapostolic criteria and what nonhistorical ways of knowing are available for this task. Surely we cannot object to the need for understanding (what Paul said), rather than mere unintelligible repetition; but what is it to criticize Paul's interpretation? Does this mean that we can amend or replace the scriptural interpretation with one of our own? That may not reduce to a "theology of decision," but it does imply the acceptance of a norm inconsistent with and independent of Scripture. By distinguishing proclamation from information, moreover, Kümmel seems to imply that proclamation contains no information, hence is not true as an account of what happened.

The predicament of the *Heilsgeschichte* scholars, therefore, lies in regarding history as an avenue of divine disclosure but suspending the meaning of that revelation upon subjective factors. If Bultmann was content to connect Old and New Testaments in decision (and even then viewed the former only in terms of negative antithesis), while *Heilsgeschichte* scholars insist on connecting them historically, the contemporary salvation-history school nonetheless compromises objective historical revelation in a manner that suspends its meaning upon personal response. The intelligibility of revelation remains a matter of private decision. The dilemma confronting this salvation-history compromise is reflected by Nils Ahstrup Dahl of Oslo: "I don't want to say that all religious affirmations are only subjective emotive affirmations, but I find it hard to state the alternative without surrendering what I want to preserve— the right of historical research to establish truth."

This bifurcation of divine revelation into a deed-revelation in history and a meaning-revelation in experience has propelled the problem of history to new prominence. In fact, the debate over the definition and meaning of history has become so technical that few scholars any longer feel wholly at home in it. In barest terms, history involves these questions: What relation if any exists between event and meaning? Does one method grasp both event and meaning? Are there bare events as such or only interpretations of historical process? What relation exists between Christological faith and historical fact?

Heinrich Ott, Barth's successor in Basel, contends that no historical facts whatever exist. Significance is an integral and constitutive element of all historical reality. Reality impresses itself upon us in the form of pictures which we interpret, and from which we abstract "facts." Hence, history, he says, is always of the nature of encounter: all reality merges factual, interpretative, and mythical elements. "God's seeing" —his purpose and goal in historical events—is said to exclude a purely subjective notion of history, and thereby limits the danger of relativism. But because we stand within history, argues Ott, we can never transfer ourselves to God's standpoint. It is through the Spirit's inner testimony that "the knowledge of faith" assures us of having rightly understood the Christ-event.

Instead of detaching historical investigation from the philosophical presuppositions of twentieth-century dialectical-existentialist theory as well as from nineteenth-century naturalism, some recent scholarship stresses an existential relation to history in which historical continuity yields to "personal-ontological continuity." Hardly surprising, therefore, is Ott's acknowledgment that "the mystery of historical reality, its ambiguity and depth" are more likely to multiply the historian's esteem and awe than to reward with striking results the axioms on which historical research is presently conducted.

Many graduate students find the current climate of conflicting exegetical claims so confusing that they are tempted to identify the "assured results" of historical research simply with "what most scholars (now) think." The definition of history remains so much in debate that more radical students think of history only in terms of historical documents plus the imagination of historians.

SALVATION-HISTORY AND ITS MEANING

Theological debate on the Continent is now especially intense between those who contend that God's redemptive revelation is historical in character and those who dismiss salvation-history as myth. The debate is marked by many compromises and inconsistencies. While a dialectical theologian like Barth deplores the vagaries of Bultmann's existentialism, his own strongly asserted "objectifying elements" remain inaccessible to objective reason and historical research. Brunner also disdains Bultmann's reduction of the New Testament miracles to myth; yet he himself rejects the Virgin Birth as mythology, depicting it as "the crucial negative idea" and contending that whoever insists on it is bound to "go wrong."

Advancing beyond the dialectical consignment of revelation to the mere margin of history, the *Heilsge-schichte* scholars emphasize historical revelation by locating divine disclosure in the very time-line of sacred events.

Cullmann views salvation-history as a revelatory activity in which God's plan is unfolded. His Basel colleague Karl Barth absorbed history into the decrees of God and emptied it of revelation-content by locating justification in creation and by viewing all men as elect in the man-Jesus. For Cullmann, the options are not so predetermined as to nullify revelation and decision in history, although Cullmann objectionably puts time in the nature of God as the means of preserving a genuine distinction between what has happened and what will happen. The concrete historical character of divine disclosure is a controlling emphasis of Cullmann's thought. God acts in the contingent temporal sphere, and divine revelation takes place in "sacred history"; at the center of this line of time, which reaches from creation to consummation, stands Jesus of Nazareth as the absolute revelation of God. There can be no *Heilsgeschichte* without Christology, and no Christology without a *Heilsgeschichte* that unfolds in time, Cullmann contends. While he emphasizes Jesus' work more than his person, Cullmann insists that one can assuredly possess authentic Christian faith only if one believes the historical fact that Jesus regarded himself as Messiah—a complete inversion of Bultmann at this point. Thus Cullmann views the history of salvation as the locus of divine revelation, anchors revelation in the dimension of historically verifiable facts, and assigns to historical knowledge a relevance for faith that is more in keeping with historical evangelical theology.

It is indeed noteworthy that Cullmann wholly rejects the reduction to myth of any link in this temporal sequence of salvation-history. Cullmann nonetheless retains the notion of myth, applying it to events beyond the time-line both past and future—events that cannot be investigated by historical method. Such are the Adam story and the events of eschatology, Old Testament and New.

Thus we come upon a curious disjunction in Cullmann's thought. While he describes such events not as actually historical but rather as myth, he concedes that the biblical writers regarded them as historical (as Christ's descent from Adam, and so forth) and therefore placed them on the same level with events on the time-line. As the biblical writers "tried to demythologize" (in Cullmann's view) in a way that extended the historical into the nonhistorical past and future, so Cullmann aims also to illumine such past and future "myths" through Christ as the midpoint of salvation-history. But Cullmann has not really reconciled this supposed misjudgment of historical realities by the biblical writers (and presumably by Jesus of Nazareth also) with the high view he elsewhere insists upon—that sacred history and its biblical interpretation are both rooted in divine revelation.

Many *Heilsgeschichte* scholars push Cullmann outside their circle, however, because—like more traditionally conservative men such as Jeremias and Michel— he speaks of Jesus' Messianic self-consciousness (a predication equally distasteful to the post-Bultmannians, Eduard Schweizer excepted). Cullmann's critics complain that his historical critical investigation is dominated by theological presuppositions—from which they presumably are scot-free in achieving contrary exegetical results!

In his newest work, *Heil als Geschichte,* Cullmann lifts the contemporary European discussion of revelation as history and revelation as truth to new and significant dimensions. He notes the "meshing of historical fact and interpretation" in Old and New Testaments and recognizes the reality of revelation both in "the event as such and in its interpretation." In the theological controversy over history and kerygma, Cullmann emphasizes a series of vital points—particularly the following: that the New Testament itself relates salvation-history to eyewitness and thus places it in a truly historical setting; that New Testament revelation not only carries forward and enlarges but also reinterprets the earlier scriptural interpretation in connection with this new saving history; that in New Testament times the revelation of new events and meanings is compressed into a much shorter time-span than in the Old Testament era, and that these divine realities now center in one person; that the New Testament reinterpretation is linked to a dual history of salvation—on the one hand to the Old Testament kerygma, on the other to the great central event along with Jesus' own kerygma about it; that the meaning of events after Jesus' death was disclosed to the apostles simultaneously with those events, not subsequently or progressively, as when they were eyewitnesses of his works; that while as eyewitnesses they saw and heard yet lacked full understanding, the later complete revelation reinterprets the kerygma so that they *remember* what Jesus himself had told them, and that this along with their eyewitnessing is of greatest importance in designating Jesus as the originator of the reinterpretation of the kerygma.

THE MEANING OF REVELATION

The *Heilsgeschichte* emphasis on historical revelation represents a development that moves beyond both Bultmann and Barth and that is as distasteful to one as to the other. Barth avoids the concept of *Heilsgeschichte,* preferring to speak instead of "the *Geschichte Jesu Christi,*" of that which "happens and continues to happen." The tendency of both post-Bultmannian and *Heilsgeschichte* scholars to resurrect the search for the historic Jesus he considers a mistake that regrettably "returns to the way of the nineteenth century." "It marks a retreat from the New Testament witness," contends Barth, "to something behind the witness and existing independently of it. I don't like the term *'Historie'* [knowledge of what has happened]," protests Barth, "and much prefer *'Geschichte'* [something that happens]." Barth's view of the role of historical investigation in relation to faith remains so negative that historical research, as he sees it, not only may lead to a false construction but *"must* yield a Jesus not identical with the Christ of the New Testament." Nonetheless New Testament scholars are increasingly pursuing exegetical and historical studies and are letting the dialectical theologians paddle for themselves.

Yet the *Heilsgeschichte* emphasis on historical revelation surrenders on the one side what it gains on the other insofar as it suspends the meaning of that revelation on spiritual decision rather than deriving it from an authoritative Scripture through historical investigation. Some *Heilsgeschichte* scholars view the truth of revelation not as universally accessible and valid for all men but, in agreement with Barth and Bultmann, as existing only for some persons in and through a miracle of grace. Thus the meaning of revelation is presumably carried not by saving history or the biblical interpretation but by spiritual decision.

Precisely at this point the young but growing Pannenberg school insists on historical revelation in a larger sense that incorporates additional elements of an evangelical theology. In his *Offenbarung als Geschichte,* a recently translated work, Pannenberg sees the denial of the objectivity of revelation as a threat to the very reality of revelation. Contrary to Barth's contentment with "objectifying" elements in dogmatics, he insists upon the objectivity of divine revelation. Pannenberg vigorously opposes the way in which the dialectical theology relates revelation and its meaning to truth and history alike. He deplores the Barth-Brunner legerdemain with the problem of revelation and history —as when Brunner says that the kerygma which brings forth faith includes history "but not in the isolation which the historian demands." It distresses him that whenever the dialectical theologians run into a historical problem they rise above it by appealing evasively to the self-communication of God.

Although he reasserts objective historical revelation, Pannenberg does not preserve the traditional distinction between general and special revelation. What has happened in time, he says, is God's revelation as such, but what has happened in Jesus Christ is the real clue to the totality of happenings. Barth criticizes this approach, contending that no such "general revelation" exists, but only a particular revelation of God's doing. Pannenberg holds that everyone stands in some relation to God and therefore has a general knowledge of God; but this knowledge he refuses to call revelation. Revelation he defines as the self-disclosure of God in the end-time (because at the end of his deeds) as realized proleptically in Jesus. In defining revelation as history, Pannenberg holds we must regain an original "eschatological understanding." On this basis he criticizes Cullmann's view of Christ at the middle of the time line of saving history, and holds instead that Christ is the end of history as fulfillment. Yet this end is at once always present and also future. Whereas Bultmann connects the Old and New Testaments in existential decision and *Heilsgeschichte* scholars connect them historically, Pannenberg relates them apocalyptically. Some *Heilsgeschichte* scholars protest that Pannenberg's main interest is *Universalsgeschichte,* or universal history, rather than salvation-history; but Pannenberg's correlation of divine disclosure with special revelation means that he, like Barth, views all divine revelation as saving. In fact, Pannenberg assertedly seeks to carry out the basic intentions of his former teacher, intentions that he thinks Barth weakened by his dialectical concessions.

RADICAL TRANSCENDENCE

The main significance of the Pannenberg plea for objective historical revelation is its open recognition that unsatisfactory formulations of the transcendence of God and of the relation between eternity and time have dominated European theology since Kierkegaard. It is noteworthy that in Kierkegaard's homeland the Copenhagen theologian N. H. Söe (who thinks SK's influence is here to stay) criticizes Kierkegaard's time-eternity disjunction as being objectionably philosophical. Kierkegaard, says Söe, finds his concept of time in Greek rather than in Palestinian motifs. Like Cullmann, Söe views time as created by God and made therefore to receive God's revelation. But Söe does not on that account view divine revelation as objectively given in history, because with Kierkegaard and Barth he understands revelation in terms of singularity and as existing for man in any given moment only as an act of grace. At this point Söe's thought mirrors SK's *Postscript.* Despite theological perpetuations of Kierkegaard's views, Kierkegaard now is little followed by European philosophers. And even among Danish theologians his positions are brought under increasing criticism. K. E. Lögstrup of Aarhus assails especially Kierkegaard's individualistic emphasis and self-centered approach to the teaching of Christian love.

Anders Nygren of Lund, whom Gustaf Wingren

groups with Barth and Bultmann in *Theology in Conflict* (1958) because of his inversion of Gospel and Law, is nonetheless a stern critic of Barth's extreme disjunction of eternity and time. "We must be done," he says, "with the docetic notions of revelation so popular in our generation." Barth found his point of departure in Plato and Kierkegaard, remarks Nygren, and he was "right in drawing the consequences, that we cannot truly speak of God" once eternity and time are over-separated this way. "But," counters Nygren, "on the basis of God's image in man, now shattered, and especially of the incarnation, we may indeed speak of God." Over against Barth, Nygren speaks of God's continuing revelation in nature, history, and conscience.

Helmut Thielicke of Hamburg assails Barth's and Bultmann's radical disjunction of eternity and time from another angle. Their approach, he says, left the Church impotent to provide a social ethic. "The Barth-Bultmann theology was unable to stimulate the ethical concern of the Church, the latter because Bultmann places everything within the individual, the former because Barth so idealizes Christ that even *Heilsgeschichte* gets lost in a 'supernatural *Heilsgeschichte*.' Hence Barth must superimpose the New Testament imperative and indicative upon his dialectical formulation." Although Barth was a strong opponent of the Third Reich, the effect of his theology, Thielicke contends, "was to call the Church to think of itself while the world was left to itself. No Christian criterion was given to the world whereby the world could judge itself. As a consequence, both the self-certainty of the Church and the self-certainty of secularism increased." Unlike Barth, Thielicke insists upon general revelation. Although man is "subjectively closed to the revelation," an ethical possibility exists different from Barth's projection—though not without its own difficulties.

Thielicke asserts that the kerygma-theologians "forget
that the objects of theology are the actions of God—
and that involves history."

THE HISTORICAL JESUS

Thus far rationalistic and irrationalistic liberalism alike
have failed to discover the authentic historical Jesus.
Both Bultmann and Barth deplore the historical critical
method as leading necessarily to a false Christ. There
is growing suspicion that not the facts about revelation
and history and faith but prior dialectical-existentialist
assumptions arbitrarily dictate this verdict.

Those who insist upon the importance of the Jesus
of history as decisive for Christian faith now follow
two main avenues—one illustrated by Ethelbert Stauffer, the retired Erlangen New Testament scholar, and
the other by the Uppsala New Testament exegetes
Birger Gerhardsson and Harald Riesenfeld. Stauffer
proceeds on the nineteenth-century notion of a fundamental break between Jesus and the primitive
Church. "I see only one way to find an objective basis
for our Christian thought and life: the question of the
historic Jesus," says Stauffer. "The historical Jesus
in the Bible is my canon." And the starting point of
this truly historical Jesus, he identifies infallibly with
"those few hundred words" where the Evangelists give
us what is a scandal to them or to the early Church.
"There they record what belongs to the historical
Jesus." While Stauffer insists that "the word, the work,
and the way of Jesus are crucial," the Swedish scholars
assail the presuppositions underlying his historical
study. "A valid methodology," protests Riesenfeld, "will
recognize the continuity between Jesus and the primitive Church." Nor are the Uppsala exegetes impressed
by a second assumption that Stauffer shares with Hans

Conzelmann, namely, that anything found in Judaism is not to be ascribed to Jesus. That is simply the myth of the total originality of Jesus, whereas Jesus is not without a point of contact in Judaism.

Riesenfeld and Gerhardsson boldly criticize one crucial presupposition of the *Formgeschichte* of Dibelius and Bultmann. In a climate of mounting criticism of Bultmann's methodology, now also joined by Roman Catholic writers (most significantly Heinz Schürmann of Erfurt, Germany), they call for a new approach that treats historical questions earnestly. Riesenfeld and Gerhardsson dispute the Bultmannian notion that one can immediately elucidate the formulation of New Testament material by applying the form-critical method. While they grant that every Gospel pericope has its life situation in the history of the primitive Church, they reject the inference that the pericope has therefore been *created* by the primitive Church. They concede further that the content has been changed and modified by the primitive Church, but they insist nonetheless that a real tradition originating with Jesus himself is included. What the Uppsala scholars demand, therefore, is a methodology aware of the firmness of this tradition.

"The Bultmannian theology is a twin sister of the form-critical view of the origin of the Gospel tradition," notes Gerhardsson. "The two presuppose one another. But I don't find that the a priori skepticism, which determines the form-critical program, is historically justified. I am trying to find a method of exploring—by way of purely historical research—the way in which the Gospel tradition was transmitted—technically speaking —in the early Church. Historical research cannot solve theological problems—in any case not all of them—but it can help theology by way of providing some firm points and basic values. And the unwarranted a priori skepticism of the form-critics can hardly serve as a basis for a realistic theology."

A SPECTER IN CONTEMPORARY THEOLOGY

A question that New Testament critics can no longer evade haunts European theology today. In Hugh Anderson's words, it is this: "What bearing or relevance for Christian faith or theology has historical knowledge that is gained from historico-scientific research?"[1]

Ever since John the Baptist's clarion call, "Behold the Lamb of God, which taketh away the sin of the world," the relation of the historical Jesus to the preached Christ has been of vital concern. In the nineteenth century, naturalistic historicism rejected the apostolic Christ as a speculative invention and professed to discover an original nonmiraculous Jesus. In the twentieth century, naturalistic scientism, reflected in the imaginative religious mood of Bultmann, commended the "apostolically proclaimed Christ" but dismissed the life, deeds, and words of Jesus of Nazareth as irrelevant to Christian faith. Whereas the old rationalistic liberalism championed the historical Jesus at the expense of the "kerygmatic Christ," its dialectical-existential successor championed the "kerygmatic Christ" to the neglect of the historical Jesus. The "witness of faith" thus replaced interest in the "facts of history"; existential experience rather than objective history became the pivot of divine revelation.

At first the new theology's description of revelation in wholly transcendent categories, independent of historical correlation, was welcomed. It seemed a necessary corrective to rationalistic liberalism's derivation of Christian realities from the socio-cultural environ-

[1]Hugh Anderson, *Jesus and Christian Origins* (London: Oxford University Press, 1964), p. 93.

ment. But theological neglect of the historical foundation of Christian belief proved costly. Preserving only an oblique reference to the bare fact of Jesus' life and crucifixion, Bultmann's existentialism ran the risk of dissolving the Christian kerygma into a Christ-myth and the Gospel into a speculative theory of existence. In defining faith as a frontier moment of repeated existential decision, Bultmann rejected the evangelical view that Jesus of Nazareth is the ground of Christian faith. And Barth, despite his tardy repudiation of existentialism and his firmer connection of kerygma with divine deeds, by distinguishing *Geschichte* from *Historie* obscured Christianity's historical foundations also. For Barth and Bultmann alike, historical exegesis is no valid avenue of knowledge concerning Jesus Christ but a faithless clinging to this-worldly props.

But the debate over the significance of the historical Jesus for Christian theology has now become a central issue in contemporary theology. By suppressing historical interest in Jesus Christ, the kerygma-theology encouraged a Docetic Christology; that is to say, it tended to reduce the Christ's presence in history to a phantom appearance. While the kerygmatic repetition that Christ is Lord held sole importance, the historical facets of the life and ministry of Jesus became irrelevant.

Present-day Christian theology can be rescued from this costly development only by a full rehabilitation of the historical realities of the Gospel. Because biblical Christianity demands an open interest in the historical Jesus, both post-Barthian and post-Bultmannian scholars now insistently raise the question of the connection or unity of the historical Jesus with the kerygmatic Christ, and the link between the teaching of Jesus and the apostolic proclamation. In their "new quest" for the historical Jesus, Bultmann's successors · struggle to establish the continuity of the kerygma with the mission and message of Jesus of Nazareth. But their use of lingering existential categories such as "the immediacy of Jesus for me" and "encounter with the selfhood of Jesus" precludes a definitive contribution to a historical investigation of the relation between the historic Jesus and the kerygmatic Christ. The "new questers" know that to dehistorize the kerygma is theologically illegitimate. But their assertion that historical aspects of the life and work of Jesus are inseparably related to the Christ of faith hangs in midair. Even some of the critics who advance beyond the Marburg mythology and the post-Bultmann reconstructions as well do no justice to the realities of historical revelation.

Is it really true, as Hugh Anderson would have us believe, that Christ's incarnation, resurrection, and ascension are events "concerning which the historian *qua* historian can really say nothing, save that a number of people came to hold belief in these things at a certain time in the course of human history"?[2] Did the Evangelists suppress their instinct for historical reality when they testified to these great events? That historical science cannot fully plumb the realities of the biblical kerygma is no reason for succumbing to negative historical criticism, or for demeaning what historical investigation can establish. To be sure, the historico-scientific method of research about Jesus cannot fully explain the psychological processes by which he was recognized as the Christ; faith-response is not open to historical study. Nor does the historical fact of the empty tomb of itself give assurance of a Risen Lord. But the sensitive historian is not so bound to an intra-worldly nexus of causes and effects that he must ascribe

---

[2]*Ibid.,* p. 60.

New Testament realities to subjective factors at the
great cost of discrediting competent eyewitnesses.

Anderson endorses Bultmann's call to rid the apostolic message of "the false scandal of the obsolete
mythological world view, ideas and language, in which
it has been clothed in the New Testament."[3] He insists that "the Bible's language about God, the world,
and history is permeated with mythological traits,"
so that "there is no escape from the task of demythologizing."[4] He ignores the contributions of conservative
scholars like Machen and Warfield to the history-and-
faith controversy, while he disparages the "uncritical
evangelicals"[5] and speaks of biblical authoritarianism
as uncritical.[6] He approves the liberal theology once
taught in American Protestant seminaries by Bushnell,
Clarke, and Brown as "deeply evangelical."[7] He prizes
the socio-historical method above a strictly historical approach to the New Testament[8] because it stresses his-
torical-human factors in the reception and interpretation of revelation and the kerygma.[9]

The merit of Anderson's book lies in its full reflection of influential theological currents, in its recognition of the crucial importance of the history-
faith problem for contemporary Christianity, in its analysis of certain weaknesses of existential exegesis, and
in its awareness of significant recent biblical studies
by New Testament scholars. But at the central point
of commentary on faith-history tensions, Anderson
fails to provide either an adequate solution or a clear
alternative. Despite emphasis on the importance of

---

[3]*Ibid.*, p. 53.
[4]*Ibid.*, p. 75.
[5]*Ibid.*, p. 76.
[6]*Ibid.*, p. 78.
[7]*Ibid.*, p. 62.
[8]*Ibid.*, p. 70.
[9]*Ibid.*, p. 75.

history for the kerygma, he reduces that history to relative importance and, in fact, leaves its range and character in doubt. Indeed, he limits the role of the historical method. The historian, he says, "may constantly protect the Church's theology from relapsing into a historical speculation . . .; he can preserve . . . the truth that our faith and our religion are rooted and grounded in a particular history and person and life; he can . . . throw some light on how Jesus' contemporaries understood him and even, to some extent, on how he may have wished to be understood."[10] But if the historian cannot, as Anderson insists he cannot, grant legitimacy to any historical grounding of faith; if he cannot authenticate any sure words or deeds of Jesus; if the records upon which he depends transform the basic historical facts of the life of Jesus; and if, moreover, faith is wholly dependent upon encounter by the Risen Christ, as Anderson also contends—then the historian's inquiry is foredoomed to irrelevance. The modern theological road often follows many welcome detours around peril-fraught landscapes. Anderson steers a non-Bultmannian course for a large part of his journey. But his observance of historical markers is hurried, and he is mainly concerned with the vision of the kerygmatic Christ. In the last analysis, Bultmann's existentialism still remains the shortest route between Spirit-faith and historical skepticism.

---

[10]*Ibid.*, p. 316.

4

Basic Issues in Modern Theology: Revelation as Truth

METAPHYSICAL PERSPECTIVES have faded from the modern scientific and democratic community. An absolute authority and an objective revelation are difficult to understand and even harder to accept. How are we to cope with this predicament? By accepting secularization? By "demythologizing" the Gospel and changing theology into anthropocentric *Existenzverstandnis?*[1] Or shall we retain traditional terms like revelation but redefine them speculatively?

"No!" replies Uppsala professor Birger Gerhardsson. Instead, he insists, we must confront the present crisis by probing these two fundamental questions in a new way: (1) What is *revelation?* (Does it or does it not contain certain "facts" and "information" which, if altered, change truth into a lie?) (2) What is divine *authority?* (Does faith involve a measure of belief in authority and specifically in *divine* authority?)

This connection of divine deed and divine information in the Swedish scholar's discussion of revelation puts a finger on the second basic issue in contemporary theology—namely, the character of revelation as truth and not simply as act.

---

[1]Self-understanding in terms of *existenz* (q.v.), or the unique individuality of the self. Although Bultmann emphasized existential self-understanding to forestall a scientific reduction of man to impersonal categories, his appeal to volitional, emotional and subconscious elements of human experience bypassed the significance of conceptual reasoning in relation to transcendent reality.

That divine disclosure occurs in history and not merely as personal confrontation or as subjective stirring on the fringe of history is increasingly emphasized over against existential and dialectical viewpoints. Conservative scholars like Adolf Köberle stress that Christianity rests on historical revelation and that God's saving disclosure is given objectively in special historical events: "In the New Testament," says Köberle, "the great deeds of God are proclaimed like news: 'The battle is finished; the victory is won; the trespasses are forgiven.' Then the reader is called to appropriate this subjectively and to realize this good news for himself. But everything hangs in mid-air if the divine events have not already taken place." So the Tübingen professor insists that in order to progress beyond its present dilemma, European theology must again recognize that *what God has done and said* is fully as important as *what God is doing and saying;* the former is, in fact, the presupposition of the latter.

This inclusion of God's *Word* in the discussion of historical revelation, and the refusal to confine it to God's Work or Act, focuses attention on the crucial question of revealed truth, which once again has become a subject of theological concern.

FROM WORD TO DEED

Admittedly, the breakdown of the dialectical *Wort*-theology[2] has encouraged a readjustment of the under-

---

[2]The "theology of the Word of God" became a descriptive summary phrase for Barth's dogmatics, in view of the appeal by crisis-theologians to divine transcendence, initiative, and disclosure—especially to the God who both acts and speaks. But the dialectical character of revelation, as Barth defined it, precluded an identification of this Word with Scripture. In contrast to the teaching of Jesus (John 10:35) and Paul (I Thess. 2:13), the crisis-theologians demeaned Scripture to "witness" to the Word, rather than recognizing it as the Word written.

standing of revelation to other categories than God's *Word*. Gerhard Friedrich of Erlangen, revision editor of Kittel's famous *Wörterbuch,* thinks that theologians in the near future will emphasize that "Jesus is Lord" more than that "God speaks." As he sees it, the Church must now locate the center of Scripture in the message that "Jesus is Lord of the world." Likewise, Ethelbert Stauffer thinks Barth too narrowly understood revelation as the *Word* of God.

To emphasize deed-revelation brings in some respects a wholesome corrective to the dialectical severance of revelation from history. Edmund Schlink of Heidelberg contends that, with its historical ingredient modified and strengthened, "the *Wort*-theology has a future."

But in other respects the *Wort*-theology represents a peak of disillusionment at the end of an era Karl Barth inaugurated with his hopeful invitation to hear the Word of God anew. As a matter of fact, the widening shift of European emphasis from *Word* to *Deed* or *Act,* in defining revelation, diminishes the intelligibility of revelation.

Although Barth's dialectical formulation precluded identifying events or concepts as revelatory, it is noteworthy that his "objectifying" additives bolstered the emphasis on revelation as truth more than the emphasis on revelation as history. In contrast with the earlier hesitation to speak of revelation in concepts and propositions, Barth today refuses to say that revelation contains no communication of information about God. Now that some European theologians are moving away from a theology of "the Word of God" toward a theology merely of "the Deed of God," Barth stresses that God's acts are not mute, and that any disjunction of Deed and Word would be "deeply nihilistic." "What would revelation mean," he asks, "if it were not an information whose goal is to be universally recognized, although not everyone recognizes it as such?"

Barth sees no hope in any movement away from a Word-theology and deplores any such development as futile. "The Word of God is the Word that is spoken by Him *in and with* His action. Act and Word belong together. God's revelation is not one of mute acts, but an Act which in itself was a Word to humanity. Any theology that disjoins God's mighty Acts from His spoken Word will ultimately prove destructive of the Christian idea of revelation itself."

REVELATION AND TRUTH

In his early writings Barth ruled out propositional statements about essential divine being on the ground of God's inconceivability. The argument was blunt: non-dialectical propositions belong to speculative metaphysics; theological ontology[3] involves the illicit objectification of God, who is unknowable and unthinkable. But in later writings Barth affirms that God is an object of knowledge: God's revelation in Christ provides a basis for genuine ontological statements. In *Anselm: Fides Quaerens Intellectum* (1931), widely regarded as a bridge between the two editions of his *Church Dogmatics,* Barth depicts faith as a call to cognitive understanding. Assuredly the 1932 revision of his *Dogmatics* reflects many passages in the earlier mood: we can know only God's acts, not his essence as such.[4] Yet in revelation we are given "a true knowing of the es-

---

[3] A later synonym for metaphysics, the term first used by Aristotle for supraphysical, hence supernatural, reality. Ontology is the science of being *qua* being, hence of ultimate being.

[4] Karl Barth, *Church Dogmatics,* Vol. I/1 (Edinburgh: T.&T. Clark, 1936), p. 426.

sence of God,"[5] a "real knowledge of God,"[6] a knowledge in terms of human cognition.[7] True faith includes
the actuality of cognition of God.[8]

Yet even in the revision of his *Dogmatics* Barth's
movement from critical to positive theology is hesitant
and halting. He places greater emphasis upon analogy
than upon dialectic. But he still disowns conceptual
knowledge of God. While "the logico-grammatical con-
figuration of meaning" is present both to belief and to
unbelief, the religious reality is present only to belief.
Theological theses are so inadequate to their object, he
contends, that no identity can be affirmed between the
propositional form and its object. Theological propositions are finally "adequate" to their object only on the
basis of an internal miracle of divine grace; theological
predications about God do not constitute universally
valid truths independent of personal decision. The correspondence and congruity of our ideas with the religious reality involves no epistemological identity between God's knowledge of himself and our knowledge
of him. All human words are "confounded by the hiddenness of God . . . and . . . in their repetition in another man's mouth they are not exempt from the crisis
of the hiddenness of God."[9]

For all his attempts to strengthen the connection
between revelation and truth, Barth's position is, therefore, still widely criticized in European theological
circles. The criticism is aimed not only at Barth's rejection of general revelation—although that is often in
view—but also at his concessions to Kantian speculation about the limits of reason, and at his suspension
of Christian truth upon private response.

[5]*Ibid.*, p. 427.
[6]*Ibid.*, p. 180.
[7]*Ibid.*, p. 181.
[8]*Ibid.*, p. 261.
[9]*Ibid.*, Vol. II/1, p. 195.

THE LOSS OF GENERAL REVELATION

Contrary to Barth's definition of all divine revelation as saving, the insistence on general revelation found expression in many theological centers in Europe. Brunner at Zurich, Althaus at Erlangen, Thielicke at Hamburg, and Scandinavian scholars as well were among those who opposed the Barthian formulation. (It is noteworthy that Pannenberg of Mainz stops short of a commitment to general revelation. Although he insists that everyone has a general knowledge of God, he does not equate this with revelation; moreover, like Barth, he holds that all divine revelation is saving.)

Over against Barth, Anders Nygren speaks of continuing divine revelation in nature, history, and conscience. He does not, however, approve natural theology, in line with the distinction that Brunner has impressed upon three decades of contemporary European theology. Nygren sees man as standing always in some relation to God on the basis of rational, moral, spiritual, and aesthetic *a priori* factors. Nygren's theological successor at Lund, Gustaf Wingren, also insists on both general and special revelation. He holds, too, that while the revelation of forgiveness (the Gospel) became known through the sending of Christ into the world and the apostolic proclamation, the revelation of wrath (the Law) is found in human life itself, independently of preaching, and that general revelation ends in the Law. Contrary to Nygren, Wingren departs from Barth's formulation by preserving the traditional sequence of Creation and Law, Gospel and Church.

But the critique of Barth's doctrine of religious knowledge does not end with the reaffirmation of general revelation. Wolfgang Trillhaas, a former student of Barth now teaching theology at Göttingen, protests that Barth so oriented theology to critical questions and to critical reason that Bultmann could readily seize the initiative. But in working out his objection to Barth's separation of revelation and reason, Trillhaas does not preserve revelation in the objective form of concepts that are valid for all men irrespective of subjective decision.

Barth himself has struggled with this problem of concepts adequate to the expression of spiritual truths. The route by which he proposes to escape agnosticism while preserving a dialectical "yes-and-no" is to many theologians both complicated and unconvincing. The dialectical theologians disparage any revived emphasis on conceptual revelation as a kind of resurrected Hegelianism. Nonetheless, the doctrine that divine revelation is given in historical events, concepts, and words belongs to mainstream Christianity; a pre-Hegelian emphasis, it has in fact been held also by ardent anti-Hegelians. Yet it is true that many post-Hegelian scholars infected this emphasis with a doctrine of radical divine immanence that violates a scriptural view of revelation. But now, in the aftermath of the equally radical doctrine of divine transcendence sponsored by the dialectical theologians, the interest in conceptual revelation is once again being explored.

THE SIGNIFICANCE OF REASON

Nygren realizes that the significance of reason is at stake in the modern controversy over revelation. "Reason is one of God's gifts to us," he remarks, "and He wills that we should use it for understanding the things in this world and for understanding Him." He disallows the dialectical premise that divine revelation is never given objectively in historical deeds, concepts, and words; instead, he holds to a normative revelation given objectively in precisely this manner, but supremely in Jesus Christ. "God is revealed in material things and in history, and He is specially revealed in biblical history and biblical concepts and words." Hence Nygren views history and concepts not merely as signposts to revelation but as the bearers of revelation. When God speaks, he speaks "in human words—and not in the twisted vocabulary of the dialectical-existential theologians." His critics, Nygren adds, with an eye on the dialectical theologians particularly, cannot argue that his view implies God's retirement, for the Spirit still "takes the revelation of God and makes it our own."

Nygren wishes, however, to avoid a "rationalistic misunderstanding" of his view and to preserve man's dependence on revelation. Curiously enough, he seeks these ends by backing away from the full adequacy of concepts for divine revelation, and deliberately stops short of the widely held evangelical view that identifies revelation in terms of propositions. "The words of the Bible are revelation, but not as propositions," he says. But this negation troubles him, and so Nygren compromises it: "We cannot press this distinction with reference to Jesus; what He says is revelation. Jesus of Nazareth is revelation. God is once-for-all revealed in the prophetic-apostolic revelation, and especially in Jesus Christ." Yet Nygren contends that even God's revelation in Christ cannot be fully captured in concepts, "not because it is inherently irrational—for it is rational indeed—but because it is too big to be captured."

The Uppsala exegetes Riesenfeld and Gerhardsson also insist on the objectivity of revelation. They move, too, beyond the *Heilsgeschichte* emphasis on deed-revelation to divine revelation in concepts and words as well as in action, and beyond this to divine revelation in Christ's words as well as in his person. They stress a special divine inspiration in the prophetic-apostolic writings and in the Church's collection of the canon.

While certain European theologians are now concerned about the significance of reason in Christian experience and about the truth-content of Christian revelation, Wolfhardt Pannenberg of Mainz is zealously formulating the case for the universal validity of revealed truth. Some Continental thinkers tend to downgrade "the Pannenberg school." Gerhard Friedrich of Erlangen refers to it as "five or six young theologians who set Hegel's philosophy over against Heidegger's, but they are already past their peak." Pannenberg is rather widely characterized as "Hegelian"—a favorite device by which many dialectical thinkers now stigmatize theologians who insist on the essential congruity of revelation and reason. The Mainz theologian rejects the label, albeit somewhat ambiguously: "I am not an Hegelian. But Hegel has been greatly misunderstood— and there is a kind of 'classical dialectic' of Hegel's to which I can be related. If we must speak of dialectic, then Hegel's is most to be respected," says Pannenberg. Bultmann views the Pannenberg movement seriously. And while he deplores any theology that does not emphasize revelation as act in contrast to revelation as objective fact, he calls Pannenberg "very gifted and clever."

UNIVERSAL VALIDITY OF REVELATION

Pannenberg's criticism of dialectical theology—be it Barth's, Brunner's, or Bultmann's—goes far beyond an insistence on objective, historical revelation. He does not, it should be said, return fully to the emphasis of historic evangelical Christianity concerning divine revelation given objectively in concept and words, nor does he identify the whole Bible with revelation. Revelation, for Pannenberg, is objective in the form of historical events, but not in concepts; while revelation does takes the form of thought, he holds it does not do so authoritatively in the special form of concepts super-

naturally given once for all, as in old Protestant theology. The Christian tradition is always in development,
he contends, because revelation is given "in deeds or
acts that remain to be explained."

But as opposed to the whole "theology of the Word"
movement, Pannenberg insists that revelation carries a
truth-claim for all men and is universally valid. He
criticizes Barth, despite Barth's theological self-correction in the area of religious epistemology, because
Barth maintains that in the final analysis the truth of
Christianity enters into the hearts of Christians only by
a miracle of grace. All the objectifying factors in
Barth's more recent dogmatics notwithstanding, Barth
remains with Bultmann "a disciple of Herrmann," says
Pannenberg; in other words, he subordinates the rational knowledge of God to trust. But if faith is in the first
instance obedience, laments the Mainz scholar, there
can be no reason for faith, nor any place for addressing
questions.

"The Christian truth is the one truth for all men,"
Pannenberg stresses, in refuting the dialectical notion
that the truth of revelation becomes truth only for in-
dividuals by personal appropriation. "There are not
two kinds of truth—one covering the arena of modern
life and thought, and the other that of Christian faith
and life and thought."

Thus Pannenberg goes also beyond the theological
milieu at Heidelberg, where he was offered but de-
clined the chair of philosophy of religion. In revelation,
both Edmund Schlink and Peter Brunner find a truth-
claim of universal validity wholly apart from subjective
decision. Brunner contends, however, that this truth-
claim is mediated not through the historical revelation
but through the means of grace. And, while he avoids
Barth's terminology, Peter Brunner nevertheless bridges
to the Barthian dialectic: "God revealed Himself in the

historical Jesus, but you cannot *prove* that He did. You cannot demonstrate revelation as a fact to one to whom revelation is not revealed. Insofar as Barth emphasizes that you cannot handle revelation as you would a loaf of bread, his position has an element of truth."

The predicament of Continental theology must be located in its unsatisfactory juxtaposition of objectivity-subjectivity, of *Historie* and *Geschichte*. But even scholars who think the objective element in revelation needs more stress than Barth assigns it often seem to yield essential terrain to the dialectical school.

With respect to revelation and reason, for example, Wilfried Joest of Erlangen insists that Christian concepts are not to be reduced simply to our own ideas about God but must include an element of universal truth, and hence constitute truth for everyman. Yet Joest emphasizes the imperfection of human concepts, wants no part of a fundamentalist view of "inspired Scriptures," and holds that God remains incognito and cannot be theoretically proved outside the phenomenon of revelation and response. He concedes there must be an existential interpretation of Christianity but of a non-Bultmannian sort, one that is "both modern and yet more congruent with the Church tradition."

The Dutch theologian G. C. Berkouwer, of the Free University, Amsterdam, asserts that "of course men can know Christ as Pilate knew Him, and Christian truth can be intellectually cognized." But it is "neither understood nor fulfilled in its real purpose apart from an act of grace." At the same time, Berkouwer thinks it unwise to reinstate the old objectivity-subjectivity antithesis and fears Pannenberg's approach may lead to a revival of natural theology. "The theological scene is now characterized by a lack of definition. What is meant by 'objective'? Surely Christian faith does not have its origin in our subjectivity. But the old objectivity-subjectivity antithesis is transcended by the fact that the Christian revelation is always 'directed' and 'kerygmatic.' God's communication always has a special purpose. We must reject the demythological facet of recent theology, but not the direction of the kerygma."

TRUTH IS TRUTH FOR ALL

In Lund, Anders Nygren forthrightly rejects the prevalent mediating notion that, while the meaning of the Christian message can be universally known, its "real meaning" can be grasped only by believers. "There are not two senses of 'meaning,' " he says. "The truth of the Christian message can be understood without personal faith. If that were not the case, all discussion with unbelievers would be impossible. As a Christian I am convinced that Christ is the Truth. He could not be the Truth, however, if He were not the Truth for all men. The truth of Christianity is universally valid for all men in all times and in all places irrespective of personal faith."

Barth, for all his effort to strengthen the adequacy of concepts for divine revelation, still insists that this adequacy exists only on the basis of recurring miracle. Revelation is "for all," he emphasizes, "but not all may catch it. The Word of God is understood only by the power of the Spirit."

Otto Weber of Göttingen, an able expounder of Barth's views, has sought to rise above the position that Christian truth exists only for the believer through grace. Divine revelation is true for the believer and also for the Church, says Weber, and *therefore* for all men. Weber complains that Barth did not connect revelation and reason "strongly enough" and insists that the dialectical theology must be developed in the direction of a more satisfactory relation between revelation and reason. Weber's larger interest is in a Christian ontology: "We cannot have theology without ontology," he asserts.

So, over against Barth, Weber contends that if revelation is indeed true, it is true for all men. "Revelation is for all but not in all and saving for all," he stresses. Does he therefore intend that the truth of revelation is given in an objective structure similar to mathematical propositions and thus valid for all men? Here Weber hedges and keeps one foot in the dialectical camp. "No man can know revelation as truth until he becomes a Christian," he holds. "Revelation is true for me as a Christian and for the Church and *therefore* for all," he continues. Theological theses are objective only because God in himself and in his revelation is "open in Christ" toward man, and is willing to communicate. In other words, Weber rejects the thesis that truth is truth for the Christian because it is universally true, and substitutes the thesis that truth is truth for all men because it is true for the Christian and the Church. Pannenberg, however, counters with the assertion that divine revelation is true for all men, and *therefore* true for the Christian and the Church.

So dawns the end of an era in which Ritschl held that the validity of religious judgments can be known only through an act of the will, in which Troeltsch found himself unable to assert the universality of the Christian religion, and in which both Barth and Bultmann failed to vindicate the universal validity of Christian revelation apart from a miracle of personal grace or an act of subjective decision. But if the deepest truth of God is found in Jesus Christ, if the contention is to be credited that Christianity is a religion for all nations, bringing men everywhere under judgment and offering salvation of import to the whole human race, then it is imperative that the Christian religion reassert its reasoned claim to universality.

CONTROLLING PRESUPPOSITIONS

Chiefly responsible for the tension in contemporary European theology is the speculative notion that divine revelation is never communicated *objectively*—neither in historical occurrences nor in intelligible propositions —but is always *subjectively* received through submissive response.

This assumption contradicts the historic Christian concept that divine revelation is objective intelligible disclosure. The classic Christian view, moreover, states that divine revelation is addressed by the Logos to mankind generally through nature, history, and conscience, and is mediated more particularly through the sacred history and Scriptures, which find their redemptive climax in Jesus of Nazareth. On this basis—of the accessibility of a trustworthy knowledge of the Living God and of his purpose in creation and redemption— historic Christianity emphasizes the possibility of personal salvation through experiential appropriation of the truth of God and of his provision for sinners. While the Holy Spirit is indeed the sole source of regenerate life and the illuminator of sinful man's darkened mind, and while faith alone is the instrument of salvation, the ground of faith—so evangelical Christianity insists— is a historical revelation and redemption; moreover, the Spirit uses God's objectively revealed truth to persuade unregenerate sinners to appropriate for themselves the saving truth and work of Christ. In a word, then, the historic Christian Church has understood divine revelation to be an intelligible, objectively given disclosure, whether that revelation be universal (in nature, history, and conscience) or special (in the redemptive deeds and declarations of the Bible).

This objectivity of divine revelation, respecting both its historical character and its universal validity, is expressly repudiated by the dialectical and existential movements in contemporary theology. In fact, the traditional "intellectualistic" view of divine revelation is deplored as a "doctrinaire" and "rationalistic" perversion of Christianity. It is ascribed to a misunderstanding of the nature of faith, which presumably is independent of a historical basis and of belief in truths about God. Not some past divine activity in the stream of objective history, nor information mediated to and through chosen bearers of God's disclosure, but rather present divine confrontation and personal response, an event here-and-now, becomes the crucial carrier of divine revelation. For more than a generation this emphasis on revelation in present-day divine-human confrontation has been the dominant theme of Continental theology, even to the extent of refashioning the doctrine of faith itself.

Much that this approach sought to correct in the many reductions of biblical Christianity needed rectification. Medieval, modern, and recent modern philosophy had all left scars upon the Christian outlook. The lamentable result was evident both in the medieval scholastic and in the neo-Protestant readiness to expound Christianity in the speculative categories of secular philosophy. It was seen, too, in the Hegelian reduction of reality to an immanentistic process in which the Absolute could be viewed only as More but never as Other, so that man's mind was exalted as part of God's mind. Other weaknesses were the modernists' loss of an authoritative Word of God in the plurality of pontifical pronouncements by their influential philosophers of religion, and the prevalent notion even in Continental Protestant churches that salvation is simply a matter of adequate catechetical instruction in Christian doctrine. Moreover, certain conservative theologians, who quite properly emphasized the propositional character of divine revelation, tended to project a schematic theology that neglected the progressive historical character of biblical disclosure. And there were those fringe fundamentalist writers who were obsessed with discovering in Scripture minute and intricate predictions of a scientific and eschatological nature. Many aspects of the theological situation might therefore have encouraged a bold, new presentation of the nature and content of divine revelation.

Nonetheless, one could have discredited and eliminated departures from apostolic Christianity without at the same time rejecting and repudiating the objectivity of divine revelation and its intelligible or universally valid propositional form. But the newer anti-intellectualistic theory of divine disclosure not only opposed certain lamentable compromises that had become current in Protestant Christianity but also proceeded to correct them by an equally egregious error. It opposed not only modern misunderstandings but also a supposed "misunderstanding" of revelation itself that virtually spanned the entire Christian era. The late Cambridge theologian J. M. Creed may have deplored the fact, but the historical actuality remains: "Had any Christian of any Church between the end of the second century and the closing decades of the eighteenth been asked a question as to the content of the Christian religion, his answer could scarcely have failed to be to the general effect that the truths of the Christian religion were contained and conveyed in the inspired books of holy Scripture. . . ."[10] In fact, this confidence in the supernatural and infallible divine communication of propositional truths is characteristic also of the New Testament writers, so that the supposed "misunderstanding" of revelation existed even in apostolic times within the dimensions of biblical Christianity. If the

[10]John M. Creed, *The Divinity of Jesus Christ* (London: Cambridge University Press, 1938), p. 105.

new anti-intellectual theory truly reflects the character
of revelation, one would have to contend that the "misunderstanding" permeates almost every portion of the
holy Scriptures! The divinely chosen prophets and
apostles, and Jesus of Nazareth too, view divine revelation in terms of revealed information about God and
his purposes. If this is intellectualistic perversion, then
not only a "doctrinaire" view of revelation but Jesus
himself and the apostles themselves must be disowned.

REVELATION REFORMULATED

The dialectical and existential *redefinition* of divine
revelation—for such it is—clearly reflects the influence of recent philosophical currents. Thus it cannot be
explained simply as a corrective reaction to recent
compromises of the Christian revelation.

Contributing to this novel reformulation of revelation were numerous speculative trends. Kant emphasized that the concepts of human reason cannot grasp
metaphysical realities and maintained that affirmations
about the spiritual order therefore lack universal
validity. Schleiermacher insisted that God communi-
cates himself but not truths about himself. Lessing
believed that no historical event can communicate
absolute meaning. Darwin taught that reflective reason
is a relatively late emergent in the evolutionary process.
Kierkegaard stressed the disjunction of the temporal
and the eternal as being so radical that only a leap of
naked faith can bridge it. Bergson declared that conceptual reasoning imposes an artificial structure upon
reality, whose rationally incomprehensible dimensions
must be grasped intuitively. There was also Ebner's
emphasis that God confronts persons only as Subject,
never as Object. And Heidegger held that reality must
be existentially experienced rather than conceptually
grasped. In one way or another, these currents undermined confidence in the ontological significance of

reason, in the rationality and objectivity of divine revelation, and in the role of cognition in religious experience.

So many and so great are the differences among the dialectical and existential theologians of our generation that should any effort be made to combine them into a single formula, one might expect an immediate disclaimer from almost all quarters. When one notes the variance between Barth and Bultmann, for example, and Barth's increasing inclusion through the years of more and more "objectifying" elements to escape an existentialized "Gospel," it might seem inaccurate indeed to view the whole dialectical-existential development as a theological monstrosity that rejects objective revelation.

But a simple test will justify classifying both the dialectical and the existential schemes in this way. However much a theology stresses "objectifying" elements, the determinative question is whether or not it views divine revelation as objectively given in historical events and in intelligible concepts and words. While the dialectical-existential theologians differ from one another at many secondary levels, they all agree in respect to this ruling notion of the nonobjectivity of divine revelation. Whether the so-called Pannenberg school projects a wholly adequate alternative may be open to serious debate; but its spokesman, Wolfhardt Pannenberg of Mainz, at least recognizes the fatal flaw in contemporary *Wort*-theology—namely, its denial of the objectivity of divine revelation and of the validity of that revelation for all men irrespective of subjective decision. A former student of Barth, the Mainz theologian considers Barth's theology, for all its "objectifying" reinforcements, unable to escape Bultmann's existentialist critique because Barth does not insist upon the objective character of divine revelation.

5

Which Way for Theology in the Near Future?

WE ARE 'ON THE WAY' in a time of great concern with crucial problems. But we do not have final answers, and I am unsure what is at the end of this theological road. Truth is our task but it is not so much our possession." So Günther Bornkamm, the Heidelberg New Testament scholar, describes the prospect for contemporary European theology and its predicament.

The role of theology in the near future is wholly unclear. Some observers wonder what trend in dogmatics will replace the dialectical theology. Others ask whether German theology may not already have forfeited its opportunity to influence postwar European thought.

THE PLACE OF THE BIBLE

Inscribed on many pulpits in Germany is the message, *Gottes Wort bleibt ewig* ("God's Word stands forever"). But the place of the Bible in the thought and life of these churches is often far less certain. Since, as Emil Brunner once remarked with unerring instinct, "The fate of the Bible is the fate of Christianity," one may rightly inquire about the Bible's status in European theology.

According to Professor Otto Michel of Tübingen, "The Bible remains the *theme* of preaching for modern theology, but it is no longer the *authority* for life and thought. Among the people generally its content is rather well-known, but it is not honored as the divine rule of faith and practice. So Germany today lacks a chart for life. It unites with other nations, but cannot supply spiritual direction for itself or for them as long as the Bible is unrecognized as the dress for the body of the Word of God."

And as far as theological students preparing for the ministry are concerned, observes Norbert Rückert, professor of studies in Nürnberg's Melanchthon Gymnasium, "the Bible is read mainly as a textbook, and all too seldom as a source of faith and devotion."

In moving from the student to the professional level in Europe, one soon discovers the source of this dominantly "academic" interest in the Bible. Even Bible commentaries tend to be more linguistic than theological, and theologians seem to select and reject their texts at will.

If, moreover, the Bible no longer ranks as an unqualified norm among most European theologians, what has replaced it?

"The norm," insists Edmund Schlink of Heidelberg, "must remain the whole canon under the middlepoint of the Scriptures: whatever points to Christ and the Gospel."

Gerhard Friedrich, revision editor of Kittel's *Wörterbuch,* disagrees. "The norm of Christianity is not the canon," he says. "Not all parts of the New Testament have the same value. Nor is it [the norm] even the center or heart of the Bible—or as Luther put it, what proclaims Jesus. It is rather [and Friedrich concedes this is time-determined] what at the time in which we live leads to man's salvation."

"The norm for me. . . ." This formula now serves to introduce not simply two, or two dozen, but a vast variety of "norms" set up by European theologians today. In fact, as many "norms" exist today as European theologians espouse for their own purposes and systems. From the ecumenical creeds to historic confessions to modern credos; from "the Absolute confronting me" to "what strikes me absolutely"; from the "Word of God" to (some of) the words of Jesus or of Scripture—the range of determinative "norms" is both striking and staggering. On any one seminary campus students usually sample but a part of this doctrinal smorgasbord; because they are free to select one or another of the proffered "norms" or even to postpone their choices, they do not experience the full discomfort and danger of such theological fare. No assessment of the present situation can hide the fact that today's multiplicity of "norms" on the seminary scene simply evidences the absence of any one authoritative standard. Aware of this awkward competition of options, European theologians no longer confidently confess what *the norm is* but rather assert what *"the norm is for me."*

Immediately after the *Wort*-theology had dethroned classic liberalism, the impression gained currency that Europe was enjoying a major theological revival. Yet it is more accurate to say that many philosophers and scientists, and most lay church members, too, have found the thinking of the theologians enigmatic, and therefore have remained quite indifferent to the theological scene.

THE NEXT TURN?

Protestant theologians on the Continent differ about whether theology should seek to be descriptive or normative. And if normative, should theology be individualistic, confessional, or ecumenical in character?

The abundance of individualistic theologies advanced by influential thinkers during the past two centuries of confessionalistic decline has encouraged two reactions: on the one hand, a movement toward *descriptive theology* (history of dogma), which rejects any aspiration to be normative; and on the other, *ecumenical theology* (whatever that may prove to be), which, it is hoped, may supply compass-bearings in the future.

Contrasted with German and Swiss theologians, who intend their theological systems (whether confessional or speculative) to be accepted as normative, Swedish theologians have quite abandoned such an ideal. Not even Gustaf Aulèn (now eighty-six years old) and Anders Nygren (seventy-five on November 15, 1965) champion normative theology, although often so represented in view of even more extreme Swedish reaction toward non-normative dogmatics. Nygren, it is true, holds to normative revelation, but not to normative theology. "There are revealed truths," he says, "but not a revealed system of truths." For him, biblical theology is the effort to grasp revelation in the form of a science. "Theology is a systematic reconstruction of revelation. There can be no genuine theology which is other than biblical—only a bad philosophy of religion. But theology is not normative; if it tries to become so, it loses its character."

A much deeper conflict characterizes the current theological scene in Sweden, however, than that posed by Nygren's distinction between scientific and normative theology. At Lund younger theologians like Per Erik Perrson and Hampus Lyttkens, who, together with the Uppsala theologians, confine their interest to descriptive theology, do so on the ground that the Bible is inconsistent and therefore cannot be normative. Lyttkens' plea for scientific theology involves also a concession to the analytic philosophy now regnant in Swedish universities, which contends that no objective propositions about God can be formulated and that religious propositions must be verified in experience.

From the perspective of this analytical philosophy the differences between Barth and Bultmann are wholly inconsequential and mainly of historical interest.

On the other hand, Gustaf Wingren of Lund, although rejecting normative theology, nevertheless insists on the biblical character of a specific theology. For this reason Nygren says that "Wingren is more normative than I." But Wingren asserts, "The fact of Christian preaching says that the Bible is normative, and modern preaching can be criticized and judged from this point of view." It is clear, therefore, that Wingren too does not believe that any one theology ought ideally to become everybody's theology. When asked how revelation ought to be defined, he gives a descriptive reply: "Revelation *in the Bible* is defined as. . . ."

Swedish theologians always place the discussion of contemporary theology in the context of the history of doctrine, and especially that of Luther-research. While their exposition of systematic theology is still presented in a way German theologians neglect and reject, it is not offered as normative—as are the theological schemes of Barth, Brunner, or Bultmann. "In Sweden the question is no longer whether a scholar stands theologically on the right or on the left," says Lyttkens (who stands considerably to the left), "but whether he is a competent research scholar."

Although theologians in Sweden have lost heart for normative theology, the New Testament exegetes at Uppsala are more cautious. Says Harald Riesenfeld, "We do not think it worthwhile to be normative at present because the theological situation in Sweden is such that no normative theology would be accepted. But we must be prepared for a new perspective; things will change in another ten or twenty years. We are inclined to think normatively because ultimately we must face the problem of truth in biblical revelation and theology."

A CHALLENGE FROM NORWAY

Norwegian theologians, however, openly challenge the prevalent Swedish assumption that theology cannot be both scientific and normative. They view the emphasis on descriptive theology or history of doctrine not simply as a Swedish tradition, which it is, but also as the by-product of the analytic philosophy dominating the universities. In Oslo, Nils Ahlstrup Dahl, New Testament professor in the Church of Norway's State Faculty of Theology, remarks that whenever the self-professed descriptive theologians preach in the churches, they forsake their detachment from normative theology. He believes that normative theology is more prominent in preaching than in dogmatic systems, which must wait for light on many problems. But Dahl's colleague, theologian Reidar Hauge, argues that dogmatics embraces more truth than sermons can, since sermons by nature cannot raise or settle many intricate questions. Norwegian theology, he stresses, is both normative and descriptive.

The Church of Norway's Free Faculty, which is more confessionalistic and less ecumenical than the State Faculty, insists even more strenuously on normative theology. "True theology must be normative," says systematics professor Leiv Aalen of the Free Faculty. "The Church in its proclamation of the Gospel must have the truth of Christ, and that will accord with the Scripture and the confessions of the Church." For Aalen the Lutheran confessional writings in the Book of Concord supply an ideal starting point in this direction. Hauge has criticized Aalen for elevating the confessions above Scripture, but Aalen denies the charge and insists that the confessions simply "protect Scripture against misunderstanding."

The abandonment of the ideal of normative theology must be traced in part to a reaction against the tide of speculative theologies; claiming to be normative, each has deluged Continental Protestantism with the influence of modern European philosophy. But this reaction against speculative theology may lead in other directions as well, such as toward a plea for a genuinely normative, authoritatively based theology. The real alternative to Bultmann's theology, contends Riesenfeld, must be "a theology authorized by the churches, a traditional Christian theology, and not the private speculations of some theologian."

The traditional conservative scholars plead for a theology whose authoritative basis is not so much established by the churches as recognized to be genuinely scriptural by the churches. Yet the loss of the biblical norm leads instead toward substitution of an ecclesiastical norm. As a result the promotion of a normative theology now tends toward two directions, one confessional and the other ecumenical.

Ideally, of course, Christian theology ought to be both ecumenical and confessional in the best sense of those terms. But at present Christendom is fragmented denominationally by competing confessions, and it is ecumenically committed in a context of inclusive theology that embraces confessional, counterconfessional, and anticonfessional elements. While member churches of the World Council of Churches have approved an elemental theological "basis," this basis serves neither as a test of doctrine nor as a deterrent to heresy.

Some Scandinavian theologians, however, feel that the Church dare not content itself with purely descriptive theological work but must crown such research with theology of a normative nature; they wistfully look to the ecumenical movement to lead the way creatively in such a development. Even those scholars who want no part of a normative theology—adrift as they are from confessional Lutheranism—are moving beyond Luther-research into new areas of dogmatic study under the aegis of their descriptive interest in history of doctrine. In Lund, Per Erik Perrson displays a growing interest in Greek Orthodox theology, and Hampus Lyttkens in Roman Catholic theology. Harald Riesenfeld of Uppsala, on the other hand, thinks the World Council might lead the way to a return to normative theology over against the subjectivistic theological speculation now rampant in Europe.

Because of the breakdown of contemporary Protestant theology, theologians in the old-line denominations are increasingly disposed to look to the ecumenical dialogue with the Eastern Orthodox and Roman Catholic churches to heal the present dogmatic ailments. Heidelberg theologian Peter Brunner believes such conversations may force a new exploration of Scripture and tradition, dogma, and other themes now overshadowed by the Bultmannian preoccupation with hermeneutics. And Edmund Schlink, who represented his church as a Vatican Council observer, predicts that through the ecumenical dialogue with Eastern Orthodoxy and Rome "new constellations will appear" to revive the themes of the Trinity, Christology, and liturgy. In the "far future" he envisions a new ecumenical theology for Christendom built on a Christological foundation; he himself is busy writing a two-volume ecumenical dogmatics. These men, Schlink and Brunner, are more ecumenical and less confessionalistic in their theological writings than are many conservative Lutheran dogmaticians, such as Walter Künneth of Erlangen and Ernst Kinder of Münster.

ECUMENICAL PROSPECTS

To date, the ecumenical development has been more hospitable to theological openness and inclusivism than to definitive dogmatics. Much ecumenical effort is based on a tolerance of wide theological differences, even upon a pragmatic impatience with theological priorities. On the Protestant side of the ecumenical movement there is little manifest indignation over alternative and competitive views. Churchmen hostile to historic Christian positions and committed to views that even the ecumenical creeds would exclude as heretical are not only defended but welcomed as divine gifts to the Church. Seminaries most energetically engaged in the ecumenical development tend to become exhibition centers for a great variety of theological viewpoints rather than bearers of an authoritatively given message.

Whether a movement that advances organizationally through theological inclusivism can also become theologically exclusive remains to be seen.

Theologian Leiv Aalen of the Church of Norway's Free Faculty is not hostile to ecumenical dialogue. Yet because of its scanty achievement to date, he does not think it will serve to reunite the churches on the basis of scriptural truth and recovery of biblical theology.

"A new estimation of Luther is necessarily emerging in Roman Catholic circles," Aalen comments, "but Rome is still more interested in involving Luther in her own system than in allowing him to oppose it in the name of Scripture. Is Rome really as much concerned about taking the Reformation seriously as about stretching its own point of view over new territory?"

Will the ecumenical direction of theology, one might ask, mean the loss of the Protestant character of the seminaries?

Schlink of Heidelberg thinks not. He feels, instead, that it will mean more serious preoccupation with the basis of the apostolic Church and with the Christianity of the first centuries in view of the ecumenical creeds.

Yet as the Protestant and Roman Catholic options are set side by side, new patterns of theological education are emerging. In Tübingen the Catholic seminar room is the first classroom that greets visitors. Munich, which has had only a Catholic faculty, failed in the effort to get Helmut Thielicke of Hamburg to serve as its first Protestant theologian, in the hope that he and Karl Rahner might occupy corresponding chairs. Hans Küng's presence in Tübingen has lent additional interest to that campus. Küng wears no clerical collar, often appears in a sport shirt, and displays Barth's writings in the front office while Aquinas' *Summa* remains in the back room. "Lourdes gives me indigestion," says Küng, who tells his classes he believes in *sola fide*. "If I were at Tübingen," a graduate student in Basel remarked recently, "I'd study under Küng; he's closer to the Reformers than Protestant theology generally." While Küng's public lectures are well attended by both Protestants and Catholics, his classes draw few Protestants, although he is credited with turning at least one of them toward the priesthood. American students in Tübingen speak more appreciatively of Küng than do German students, who consider Rahner the truly intellectual source of the ecumenical development but Küng primarily its spokesman.

Karl Barth thinks this proliferation of European theology into descriptive, confessional, and ecumenical options offers no hopeful prospect. He points to Bishop John Robinson's *Honest to God* ("at once descriptive, since he was a scientist; confessional, since Robinson is Anglican; and surely ecumenically-minded") as a clear indication that the alternatives run far deeper. "In this renewal of Feuerbach, of a theology identical with a certain kind of anthropology," says Barth, "we stand at the end of the whole development of modern theology in a return to the nineteenth century. The real question for the future of theology is this: Is there a theology not anthropological but 'theanthropological,' one grounded in the Word of God in Jesus Christ?" Barth declines to venture a prophetic verdict on the outcome: "I cannot prophesy what the general trend of theology will be—whether theology will take 'the good way' or not."

Concerning the Vatican Council dialogue, Dutch theologian G. C. Berkouwer of Amsterdam's Free University says: "The contacts are many, and Rome has able men in all fields. But to speak now of a theology of the Word of God is only a beginning. We have had this formula for over thirty years, and many accept it who destroy its best sense. It does not of itself solve the hermeneutical problem which faces both Rome and Protestantism. To face this problem is not a matter of 'unbelief'; if we do not face it, we shall be out of touch with our responsibility as well as with modern thought and life. We are called to a Gospel-conforming theology made concrete in our life work and renewed day by day."

THE PULPIT AND THE PEOPLE

The gulf separating the leadership and the membership of the Continental churches remains a conspicuous feature of the times.

One observer has said that while 95 percent of the European church leaders are increasingly occupied with ecumenical concerns, 95 percent of the church members couldn't care less.

Whatever measure of theological renewal was stimulated by the "theology of the Word of God," its con-

trolling presuppositions were too abstruse and enigmatic to prompt any great revival among the laity.

Barthian theology did indeed stimulate a new search-
ing of the Bible, and here and there it raised up powerful pulpiteers like Walter Luthie in Berne, who drew
large audiences. A significant number of European theological professors are also outstanding preachers and
fill the churches in which they minister. One might
name Thielicke of Hamburg, Von Rad of Heidelberg,
Schweizer of Zurich, Zimmerli of Göttingen, among
others—men certainly of divergent theological perspectives.

But in the main there has been no great popular
movement toward the churches in Germany and Switzerland. Not even on Christmas and Easter Sunday
will one find more than 4 or 5 percent of the church
members in attendance. Some pastors actually no longer
expect adults to attend church, although they do expect
children to go through the routine of baptism and confirmation. The man in the street—and that is where
most Germans are on Sunday—considers theological
reflection irrelevant to his most pressing concerns. In
the United States, on the other hand, people tend to
regard theology as dispensable because they attend
church in significant numbers.

In Europe the churches themselves often perpetuate
a mood of theological compromise among the few
members who do attend. Many of the Continental
churches deliberately "balance" the theological tone of
the pulpit by maintaining two pastors, one liberal and
one conservative, in order to satisfy both elements in
the congregation. The seminaries have long practiced
this approach by engaging professors of divergent theological viewpoints (although conservative replacements
seem ever less tolerable to nonconservative majorities).
Even if theological faculties have learned to live in

peace in the midst of extensive dogmatic differences, laymen still somehow expect a close relation between theology and truth. Says Professor Gerhard Friedrich of Erlangen, "One must practice theology critically. Both orthodox and liberal theology are heretical." Such a comment, while it may not startle a seminary campus, is upsetting enough for the man in the pew to make him cast all theology aside.

One disturbing factor in this confused and spiritually moribund situation is that seminary faculties seem to cultivate theology "for its own sake." Professors often insist that they are training theologians, not pastors. Thus the chronic separation of church and theology continues and worsens. Increasingly distressed over this condition, some Lutheran bishops want seminary faculties to be more answerable to their bishops. But such a prospect the university-related faculties regard as intolerable.

With most of the people "in the Church" but few of them "in the churches," the spiritual condition on the Continent is especially dark because of the widespread skepticism that there really is a Word of God that the Church must proclaim. Theology and Church, after all, must stand in some sort of reciprocal relation. And in the present situation the masses consider church attendance just another fragmentation of their time. Lutheran Bishop Hanns Lilje of Hannover has charged that Europe is no longer aware of the importance of the Bible in the conduct of human affairs; even a "simple knowledge" of the Bible, he says, is fast disappearing from European life. He is convinced of the connection between the contemporary theological situation and the breakdown of interest in Scripture: the current trend of European biblical scholarship, he insists, has "made the Bible appear to be uncertain of its message." Nor is the Bible being read in a great many homes in Germany. Yet, as Norbert Rückert of Nürnberg comments, "while the Bible is widely neglected in Protestant circles, the Roman Catholic Church has undertaken to promote a Bible-revival."

What is more, Bultmann's aim to accommodate Christianity to the modern scientific mind by demiracle-izing the Gospels has not succeeded. In point of fact, he has diverted more young theologians from biblical Christianity than he has won scientists to Christian faith. It is remarkable that among graduate students in Germany one can hear students even of Missouri Synod background contend that in every generation the Church needs a heretic like Bultmann to speak "for faith" to those outside its orbit. Yet the lamentable gulf between European scientists and theologians remains and has not been spanned by theological concession to scientific naturalism. The movement away from miracles is still mainly a movement away from the Church as well. Growing disbelief in miraculous Christianity may be assumed in the Church Free Society's claim to have liberated its almost 100,000 members from "the Church and its dogmas." The society seeks "independently thinking people" who now "belong to a church and cultural association only because of inherited custom and family tradition."

No doubt many persons who lack vital personal faith are found in Continental churches that automatically incorporate children into their membership. But it is specious to argue from this situation that Christian realities lack any sure foundation and that science brings freedom while the faith of the Church means bondage, and to convey the impression that modern science and an atheistic world view demand each other. Yet for a generation the premise that the Christian Gospel requires no break whatever with a naturalistic view of science and history has had the enthusiastic support of Bultmannian theology. The Church Free Society sponsors public lectures promoting an atheistic *Weltanschauung,* holds independent marriage, confirmation, and children's dedication ceremonies, and substitutes a light or sun festival on December 21 for the Christian celebration of Christmas.

In surveying the theological situation in Europe, one is left, therefore, with some clear impressions.

European Protestant theology has neither closed nor bridged the wide gap between the churches and the masses. The broad disagreements of the dogmaticians support the general opinion that theology is a matter of specialized speculation. Efforts to attract the intellectuals by diluting the Gospel have failed; Bultmann's demythology has won few existential philosophers from Heidegger's atheistic camp and few naturalistic scientists; moreover, those who have been influenced have yet to be won to biblical Christianity. The common people find theology too abstract and unclear for profitable reading, and church attendance they regard as sadly unrewarding. That no one norm any longer controls the climate of conviction in the seminaries is widely reflected in the pulpits, and the well-known tendency of the professionals to compromise the Scriptures as the rule of faith and life discourages Bible reading among the laity. Swedish theologians think that the whole notion of a normative theology should be discarded, but most confessional theologians believe that without normative theology the Church would go into bankruptcy.

But then again the ecumenical development is convinced that the assorted denominational confessions by which the disunity of Christendom is perpetuated cannot all be true. The resultant interest in the ecumenical movement, therefore, is supraconfessional and theologically inclusive, yet at the same time wistfully normative. Any theological norm for the ecumenical development, it now seems, will be ecclesiastically decided rather than biblically determined. The World Council of Churches, which has already forsaken its pan-Protestant character for a merged Protestant-Orthodox image, is moving into conversations with Rome at a time when the council lacks a clear theological norm and when many Protestant dogmaticians reject a Bible-bound theology. Protestant participation in the dialogue with Rome is driven forward not so much by confident theological consensus and conviction as by an exasperating lack of such concurrence, and by the secret and perhaps strange hope that larger ecumenical conversations will shape a new unity in which Protestant consciousness can survive unhindered.

JUDGMENT OF THE THEOLOGIANS

Protestant Christianity no longer responds to any one final authority. The sad result of its theological defection from the biblical norm shows in the chaotic condition of Continental religious thought. For the third time in a century the supposed bulwarks of Protestant theology are falling and scholars are seeking new strongholds.

Many questions are being asked in Europe, some of them of special interest and significance for America. What future remains for the "theology of the Word of God"? What theological development and progress can be expected in the days ahead?

But, preoccupied only with each other, the theologians seem wholly unaware of their fading prestige in the world of thought.

Is this chaotic condition in contemporary theological thought a sign of God's judgment upon the theologians? Has their persistent compromise or sacrifice of the message of the Holy Scriptures made them victims of their own confusion?

Theologians frequently remind us that divine judgment must "begin at God's house," a theme well-entrenched in modern dogmatics. Could it be, however, that they themselves have overlooked one of the subtler points of the biblical message—namely, that even theologians are not exempt from God's scrutiny?

When theology was queen of the sciences, theologians recognized the indispensability of Jesus and of the apostles for understanding contemporary man (theologians included). But now that modern theologians have made *themselves* indispensable to the "understanding" of Jesus and the apostles, theology has become the slave of speculators. What God may be proclaiming in the history of our times is that modern theologians and their theology are quite unnecessary for the well-being and ongoing of His Church.

Many theologians on university-related faculties seem oblivious of their fallen status; they seem unaware that their colleagues no longer give them the same academic esteem that scholars in other disciplines enjoy. One reason for this demotion is the apparent inability of modern theologians to communicate their convictions intelligibly. It is true that the frequently changing frontiers of dogmatics now necessitate conquering novel terrain with countless hazards of discussion. Nonetheless the physical scientists escort their colleagues over equally devious paths and do so successfully. This leads some academicians to ask whether the theologians—in the midst of their strongly asserted individualistic preferences—are perhaps using ambiguity to conceal their insecurity.

It is not only simpletons who cannot understand these theological subtleties but also some other scholars, whose own fields of specialty are highly complex; they stand amazed in the presence of the verbiage concealing Jesus the Nazarene.

But we do not believe that the theologians are deliberately clouding the atmosphere. Amid the confusion they have brought about, they are simply trying to market what is nonintelligible; that there are few takers in acadamic circles should surprise no one. Is it perhaps a sign of divine wrath and judgment that the theological leadership of major denominations is wielded predominantly by those who are content with changing fashions of doctrine, or who establish these changing fashions? The fundamental question for the cult of the professional theologians is simply this: What is God saying to them, to the theologians, who claim to be specialists in what He is saying to others? What is God trying to teach them in the historical fact that Protestant theology is suffering its third collapse in the twentieth century? Is He telling the theologians that *they no longer know what the Word of God is?*

As the religious thinkers of Europe look into the near future, what do they anticipate? While a few scholars wonder if German theology is approaching an era of divine chastisement, apparently none senses that judgment may already be in process. "It is likely," thinks Adolf Köberle of Tübingen, "that in a short time dark events and judgments of God may come over us. The future of European theology hangs heavily on events in world history."

The future, says Emil Brunner, is "a matter of the Holy Spirit. Bultmann does not even acknowledge the legitimacy of the term; for him the Holy Spirit belongs to 'the myth.'" "Communism," continues Brunner, "is still the greatest and most powerful ideological opponent of Christianity. Truth does not play a role in Communism, and totalitarian power can do away with theology."

Most scholars abroad look for a generation of action and reaction in the realm of religious thought, a time of adjustment and readjustment, of combination and recombination. The course of European theology has been determined in the past so largely by the prevailing winds of philosophical speculation that Tübingen professor Otto Michel says candidly: "No man can predict the future. Spiritual developments are rooted deeper than the theological emphases of the professors. Yet they hang together with the philosophical currents and cultural and historical phenomena which often prove decisive."

No new philosophical current as powerful as Hegel's or Kant's or Heidegger's has appeared on the German horizon. The voices of Moses and Isaiah, of Jesus and Paul are permitted to say only what the critics allow. Younger theologians evidence a rationalistic drift to philosophy of religion. No clear alternative to the broken Bultmannian perspective is yet in view. While a few strong voices are rising, each distinct from the others, none speaks comprehensively and influentially enough to warrant recognition as an established alternative to Bultmann.

One thing is clear, however. No one anticipates a golden era of theological prosperity in Europe. The conservative scholars on the seminary faculties are a woeful minority, and are often isolated. Thus any decisive shift in the outlook of Continental theology is less likely to issue from an evangelical counterthrust than from some novel philosophy. As a successor to Heidegger's *existenz,* such a philosophy may accommodate Christian motifs to new forms of speculation. Or in a context of some dark turn in European history it may either plunge the Continent into bleak despair and unbelief, or prompt men in their anguish to seek afresh the God of the Bible.

Predictions concerning the future of theology differ in perspective and intensity. "The dialectical theology is secure," says Rudolf Bultmann, despite its present turbulences, "and it has a future." Wilfried Joest of Erlangen, who agrees that the division of Bultmann's empire need not signal an end-time for dialectical theology, notes, however, its drift toward more extreme positions: "The Bultmann school is separating into diverse shades of emphasis. . . . It assumes even more radical forms among some of the Mainz professors." According to the Göttingen New Testament scholar Joachim Jeremias, "the hopeful sign and promise of a fruitful future in German theology exists through the evident turning from Bultmann's presuppositions. We must now labor as carefully as we can to get at the words of Jesus and the content of his message."

Two others, individualistic enough to preclude their attachment to any school of thought, should also be quoted here: Ethelbert Stauffer of Erlangen, now retired, and Helmut Thielicke of Hamburg. In these next years, says Stauffer, who is sometimes pictured by other New Testament scholars as "a twentieth century Renan, though not so sentimental," "the Church will find it necessary to stand in the forefront of all human concerns, and we shall see the rise of a new Christian humanism." "In 1916," he observes, "Barth's *Römerbrief* said a *nein!* to *humanismus*. The Nazi era divided Church from *humanismus* and Hitler fought both and conquered. What is needed now is not Khrushchev's socialistic humanism but a new Christian humanism in which the Good Samaritan can lead us on." Thielicke hopes that the present dead-end street in dogmatics will encourage new interest in the widely neglected realm of theological ethics: "The crisis of modern preaching lies in the fact that it speaks only to the 'inner man,' instead of addressing his socio-cultural situation."

Yet in one major respect the present age of European religious thought differs from the recent past, and particularly from the generation that Barth called to a fresh hearing of the Word of God. This new generation is the one that has already heard the summons to "the God who reveals himself" and yet has turned away to Bultmannian and post-Bultmannian positions.

What will be the plight of a future generation whose spiritual confusion is compounded by the fact that the Barthian "rediscovery of special revelation" and the message that God *speaks* is for it an already bypassed option?

While Barth's *Wort*-theology crumbled the defenses of the old liberalism, the new liberalism traces its own ancestry to the *Wort*-theology! What is the destiny of those who meet the plea for special revelation with deliberate detachment, who reject it as an incoherent and unconvincing option of dialectical theology?

Otto Weber of Göttingen captures the sorry mood in this observation: "Bultmann stressed *that there is* a Word of God even if he was unsure *what* it is. Bultmann's students all speak about 'the Word.' But now we are already seeing a movement away from the certainty *that there is* such a Word."

"Sometimes I fear the end of Protestantism in such a generation," confesses Köberle of Tübingen. "But in a dark hour, many may long again for a firm foundation and for living bread" and by God's grace "ears may be open again to *the old unshortened Gospel.*"

At present the prospect of a rediscovery of "the old unshortened Gospel," by the theologians at least, does not seem very bright, for the chaos of contemporary theology rests in the frontier realm of the problem of religious knowledge. It is a strange fact of modern

European theology that while most of its theologians stress special divine disclosure, they differ woefully as to its nature, content, and significance.

"The basic problem remains Christology," insists Wilfried Joest of Erlangen. "The real issue is the meaning of the person of Christ for the Word of God, for truth, and for justification. Is He only the prophetic mouth of God, or is he present in the Word?"

But what is this Word? Notes Peter Brunner of Heidelberg: "If the Church does not experience a new awakening—not necessarily in the eighteenth or nineteenth century sense of pietistic renewal—then we shall not have a real renewal of theology. The prophet Amos speaks of a time when people go through the land and ask for the Word of God and there will be no Word of God. This bad situation must be turned by God's grace into a good situation, or there is no hopeful future for German theology."

6

The Evangelical Outlook on the Continent

IF ONE FACT IS CLEAR from the twentieth century, it is that evangelical Christianity gains nothing from a 'reaction theology'! Because it falls short of a full biblical emphasis, 'reaction theology' is powerless to confront the alternatives and always proves weak in the next generation."

So comments the Dutch theologian, G. C. Berkouwer. One of the real tasks of evangelical Christianity, he feels, must be to move beyond old boundaries to new frontiers of theological enterprise. "The distinction between theological conservatism and progressivism is no longer serviceable," Dr. Berkouwer says. "The words are no longer useful because everybody wants to 'conserve' and to 'progress.' Lack of progress is no characterological feature of our theology. We need to face the future unafraid. Faith need not fear in the face of danger. An openness in confronting modern problems in the wrestling of this century will not destroy or dilute the Word of God, but rather will give it free course."

From another quarter—L'Abri Fellowship in Switzerland, where Francis Schaeffer works with intellectuals on the agnostic fringes of modern life—comes another warning to evangelical forces. "For many of 'the doubters' in our generation the accepted religious vocabulary no longer conveys what the words were intended to mean. So the 'general evangelicals' are often articulating slogans rather than communicating ideas.

They need therefore to step into the twentieth century."
"Worse yet," says Schaeffer, "some segments of the
evangelical movement have fallen prey to the irrationalistic spirit of the age, and they see no real possibility
of intellectual answers. They are losing a battle they
do not even realize they ought to be fighting. They give
away key chunks in their armor to the existential and
dialectical philosophies, and rely on piety and zeal to
win the day. Or they combat the new theology on too
narrow a strip—not seeing its connection with the line
of despair that characterizes modern thought."

These tendencies—first, a ready reliance on reaction-
ary negation rather than on the counterthrust of creative biblical theology; and second, a spirit of accommodation that simply erodes elements of Christian
belief less rapidly than more radical views—largely
account for the present predicament of evangelical
theology in Europe. The collapse of rationalistic liberalism in European theological thought was forced not
by traditional evangelicalism but by the crisis-theology;
it was the lack of a vigorous evangelical theological
thrust relevant to the spirit of the times that furnished
Barth and Brunner their opportunity to speak in the
name of biblical theology. Now that the existential-
dialectical framework is increasingly strained and a
search for new alternatives is under way, the question
arises whether European theological history will again
neglect a sound evangelical option—and if so, why.

There is little doubt that evangelical scholarship on
the Continent is less formidable today than in earlier
times of struggle against modern critical theories. In
German theology there have been traditionally two
streams of conservatism in biblical-exegetical scholarship. First, there was the confessionalistic theology
centered throughout the nineteenth century in the
conservative Erlangen *Heilsgeschichte* school. (Paul

Althaus, who also reflected the influence of Martin Käh-ler, carried this witness forward into the present generation.) The second trend, the pietistic movement, has taken two directions. Originating in Halle, where leaders like Francke and Tholuck combined Lutheran theology with pietism, one stream claimed Martin Kähler and Julius Schniewind among its significant figures, and in our generation has Otto Michel of Tübingen, one of Europe's able New Testament scholars, as its outstanding representative. Another stream, which under A. Schlatter combined Reformed theology with pietism, has Karl Rengstorf of Münster and Adolf Köberle of Tübingen as leading present-day exponents—the latter reflecting also the influence of the late Karl Heim, another representative of this movement.

Almost all these lines of thought have been somewhat influenced by historical criticism. Moreover, even in their dissent from dialectical theology, they have in recent years found some reinforcement in the writings of Barth and Brunner, so that some evangelical indebtedness to the crisis-theologians cannot be denied. It is true that former Erlangen giants like Hermann Sasse and the late Werner Elert took the position that what was valuable in Barth could be found in the Bible and what was false—including the dialectical structuring of theology—should not be commended to divinity students. Although Elert once said he wanted "no piece of bread" from Barth, the younger conservative theologians acknowledged a debt to Barth for his bold assault on rationalistic modernism, for his role in the *Kirkenkampf* against Nazi socialism, and for occasional fresh insights into biblical positions. In fact, in their struggle against modernism the conservative forces had to draw much of their ammunition from Barth, because their own theological leadership in the Protestant faculties had been decimated. Thus it developed, as one evangelical put it, that "Barth injected a dose of quinine into the blood of the theologians, and while this checked much feverish speculation, it also encouraged them to survive by means of dialectical infusion." This turn of events explains why any checklist of evangelical stalwarts in Europe almost invariably includes the names of scholars whose moderate adjustments to biblical criticism or accommodations to recent theology set them apart from American fundamentalism. It accounts also for the mood of moderation in conservative critiques of dialectical theology, as reflected in the works of Althaus. The list of evangelical spokesmen, therefore, is often enlarged beyond the nondialectical theologians to include scholars like Peter Brunner and Edmund Schlink of Heidelberg, whose formulations retain a dialectical structure, or Helmut Thielicke of Hamburg, who resists the Barthian theology but whose preaching and popular writing seldom reflect his full critical viewpoint.

The evangelical critique of dialectical theology has nonetheless been maintained along several lines. There is the continuance of the Erlangen salvation-history tradition by Althaus and now by Walter Künneth. The Tübingen line of Schlatter and Heim is continued by Adolf Köberle. There are the biblical exegetes specializing in Judaistic studies (Gustave Dahlmann, Hermann Strack, Otto Michel, Paul Billerbeck, Joachim Jeremias, Karl Rengstorf), and there are also some younger theologians (among them Hans Schmidt, docent for systematic theology in Hamburg, and Adolf Strobel, privatdocent in New Testament at Bonn) who criticize on biblical grounds the philosophical presuppositions of the new theology.

The difference between the conservative and mediating camps, therefore, tends sometimes to become merely a difference of emphasis. Jeremias warns, for example, against drawing too sharp a line between the traditional conservative scholars and the *Heilsgeschichte* scholars. In part, this plea springs from the fact that, although they resist extreme critical positions, many conservatives are not averse to accepting moderate critical views. So Jeremias assigns *Formgeschichte* the role of distinguishing "Palestinian from Hellenic layers" in the New Testament. But the plea is based also on the validity of the fundamental concept of salvation-history, to which the recent *Heilsgeschichte* movement does less than justice. European conservative scholars have learned not to discard valued terminology just because somebody temporarily cheapens it. "The old way, the *Heilsgeschichte* approach, was correct," Jeremias insists. "The method did not put the stress on the anthropological side but on the theological. It regarded the main task of hermeneutics as the understanding of the message of our Lord himself with the help of the biblical-Palestinian environment. It took the message of the Gospel without imposing external philosophical presuppositions."

Then too, the *Heilsgeschichte* school itself includes an exegete as conservative as Oscar Cullmann, whose theologically positive views embarrass some salvation-history scholars. In fact, just this extensive theological diversity within the modern *Heilsgeschichte* movement is one feature that differentiates it from the conservative camp. The salvation-history scholars are actually less unified in perspective than their mutual interest in historical revelation might indicate. They represent a wide variety of viewpoints and interests, although at this present time in the theological debate they manifest a common concern. Eduard Schweizer of Zürich is really a post-Bultmannian, Ulrich Wilckens of Berlin is numbered in the Pannenberg school, and Eduard Lohse of Berlin reflects much of the position of Jeremias, his former teacher.

WANTED: A NEW METHODOLOGY

Amid the growing recognition of the methodological crisis in European theology, conservatives venture little radical criticism of the presuppositions now dominant. It is doubtless true that, as Emil Brunner remarks, "the methodological alone has never changed the church line; the theological is decisive." Yet in almost every camp some scholars now recognize that the presently controlling methodological premises are under great strain because of the chaotic condition of Continental theology. The Bultmann devotee Hans Conzelmann aptly describes the present tumult as "a trouble of methodology." And Werner Kümmel, spokesman for the *Heilsgeschichte* scholars, unhesitatingly calls for "a new methodology" to replace the Bultmannian misconception of the task of hermeneutics with a renewed interest in what the New Testament actually teaches. Yet even among the more conservative scholars there is little evident disposition to attack *Formgeschichte* in more than a general way.

Whatever criticisms are sounded, however, are significant and include a rejection of Bultmann's premise that the form-critical method immediately elucidates the formation of the contents of the New Testament. Otto Michel of Tübingen has spoken openly of the need for a new and different methodology, and calls for a scriptural rather than a critical norm. While in New Testament criticism Michel confessedly retains much the same methodology as Bultmann, he emphasizes the historical roots of early Christian phenomena and achieves a theological result that is evangelically sturdy. "It is customary to draw certain contents (kerygma) from the Bible," he notes, "but not to draw categories of thought from the Bible, nor to check our categories of historical criticism from it."

A somewhat similar complaint can be found in the writings of A. Schlatter, whose untranslated criticism of modern philosophy from Descartes to Nietzsche should be better known.

DIFFICULTIES FACING CONSERVATIVES

One reason for the limited initiative and impact of conservative scholars is that their representation on the university faculties is in meager disproportion to the theological outlook of the generality of Lutheran and Reformed church members. For this reason some mainstream ministers and churches are increasingly disposed to establish centers of theological learning independent of the universities. They complain that conservative forces are not adequately represented. They charge that on retirement conservative scholars are replaced by nonconservatives. Only here and there does an isolated scholar make a mark for the evangelical cause. Among such is the New Testament professor Johannes Schneider, a Baptist, recently retired from Humboldt University in East Berlin.

Time pressures on the conservative scholars are such that their literary output often lags. Moreover, the theological situation often requires their engagement on a more technical level than polemical debate. Yet Barth, Brunner, and Bultmann all knew the value of closely reasoned textbooks supporting their positions. A time of theological transition requires coping with the concerns that engage the influential theologians. If evangelical Christianity is again to acquire mainstream theological power, it cannot perpetuate itself by remaining in ideological isolation from dominant trends of thought. Furthermore, the paucity of conservative theological literature frustrates evangelical students. Because there is little else, the dogmatics of

Barth and Brunner, appropriated critically, serve as the main theological supply of many conservative students, while Von Rad's Old Testament theology fills much the same vacuum in that area. Yet the picture is not wholly dark. A few valuable works have appeared from the conservative side, among them Michel's commentaries on Romans and Hebrews. Long a publishing house for pietistic literature, Brockhaus Verlag in Wuppertal has now widened its program to include the publication of theological works.

In a campus atmosphere of many viewpoints, students easily become skeptical of theological truth as something beyond their reach; instead, considerations of professional status and ecumenical eligibility bulk large. Even if the diversity of faculty perspectives does not result in the systematic destruction of their faith, evangelical students still must "struggle not to be drowned," because conservative scholarship on the Continent lacks dynamic centers for comprehensive propagation of its convictions.

Almost a century ago there was a great debate over whether evangelical isolationism rather than evangelical penetration would result from the participation of evangelicals in Free University, Amsterdam. The only Calvinistic university in the world, it has registered growing influence in shaping a task force of conservative scholars. It is clear that in the seminaries at German universities no community of evangelical scholarship has arisen and that evangelical forces have been largely isolated from the ecumenical dialogue, which mainly reflects what is currently fashionable. While the traditional conservative scholars did not gain a large platform in Germany during the Barth-Bultmann era, it is noteworthy that Rengstorf, Michel, and Jeremias have been popular guest lecturers in Sweden. Discussion of demythology and of dialectical theology has been more marginal in Sweden than in Denmark, which has been aligned mainly on the Barthian side.

In the past century, as rationalistic liberalism began to pervade the seminaries, Bible institutes were established within the state church framework. Among these were *Missionsbibelschule Liebenzell* in the Black Forest, which now enrolls sixty students annually, and St. Chrischone near Basel, which has eighty students and became quite widely known through Fritz Rienecker's writings.

But doctrinal dilution is a problem not only of the university theological faculties; most free church seminaries also reflect a considerable measure of theological diversity. They make little decisive contribution to the main currents of European theology. Their literature program rests upon too few professors. Even the well-equipped Southern Baptist seminary in Ruschlikon outside Zürich is being strengthened against criticisms of mixed position on the inspiration of the Bible and against some past intrusion of Barthianism into its theological emphasis.

Although evangelical scholars in Europe readily support on scriptural ground their conservative positions against dialectical theology, they are more timid about turning their theological presuppositions into a vigorous counterattack. As a result their work tends more to demonstrate the inadequacy of Bultmann's, Barth's, and Brunner's deformed dogmatics than to formulate a comprehensive alternative that grapples with problems posed by contemporary theology.

It is significant that evangelical scholars in America have formulated their objections to neo-orthodox theology more extensively and more fully than have European conservatives. Yet the writings of Gordon H. Clark, Edward John Carnell, Cornelius Van Til, Paul K. Jewett, and other critics of neo-orthodox theology are largely unknown or are brushed aside on secondary grounds. German theology, for all its comprehensive character, is actually very provincial; in many respects it is a closed corporation indifferent to foreign competition and comment. An exception is G. C. Berkouwer's constructive critique of *The Triumph of Grace in the Theology of Karl Barth,* which has been translated from Dutch into German and of which Barth has taken appreciative but unrepentant note. But as a general rule, notes an American observer, unless outside comment comes from a Germanic name like Niebuhr or Tillich, it will be ignored as theologically insipid. And if it comes from conservative sources, it will be overlooked as dealing with questions of no special interest to European theologians.

This tendency to ignore conservative Protestant thought is not particularly German; it is characteristic of liberal Protestantism in general. Contributors to the recent work *The Historical Jesus and the Kerygmatic Christ* simply ignore the painstaking American efforts in historical research by J. Gresham Machen and B. B. Warfield in New Testament studies or relevant work on the British side by men like James Orr and James Denney. Dr. John Baillie, the late principal of New College, Edinburgh, and a gifted scholar in his own right, once rejected a proposed assessment of Orr's writings as the subject of a doctoral dissertation on the ground that Orr was "not really a scholar." The prejudice that biblical Christianity cannot and will not be defended by a true scholar is a widespread denigrating notion in some liberal circles. Actually, however, it merely reveals the illiberality of liberalism. The reading and reference lists in ecumenical seminaries and the books proposed for translation by ecumenical literature committees reflect much the same temper, as do the reviews in such journals as the *Journal of Bible and*

Religion, the *Journal of Biblical Literature,* and indeed, the *Christian Century.*

PIETISTIC CONCERN

European church life also includes a pietistic force, one alertly evangelistic and concerned with the practical side of the Church's mission. Although it, too, deplores the impact of Bultmann upon German church life, its opposition is more polemical than comprehensively dogmatic. Its most conspicuous achievement has been the sponsorship under the German Evangelical Alliance of large-scale evangelistic crusades in which evangelist Billy Graham has called the masses in major German cities to faith in Christ. The alliance is an organizational rallying point for conservative leadership from both the people's church and the free churches. It has also sponsored community evangelistic efforts by the Janz Brothers, Gerhard Bergmann, Anton Schulte, and others. At the level of the local churches the German Evangelical Alliance has exerted a formidable influence for spiritual renewal. In Paris, encouraged by a similar French group, more than 200 pastors and workers now attend an annual three-day conference of evangelical leaders from French-speaking countries.

Unfortunately, the evangelical witness is impeded by a lack of coordination of independent and interdenominational efforts that cling to desires for private glory; nevertheless, greater association among leaders of diverse projects is noticeably increasing. The strength of independent evangelical effort still lies in its vigorous appeal to the God of the Bible expounded in an unqualified way. "We are not surprised," says René Pache of *Institut Emmaüs,* Lausanne, "when neo-orthodox positions crumble, since even those theologians who revived a theology of 'the Word' insist that the Bible is not the Word of God." The task, he adds, is "not to create a competitive new theology, but to train a ministry concerned for a full hearing and full obedience of God's Word."

The conservative Bible schools in Europe, however, tend to move outside the theological dialogue. Most faculty members feel that the debate as now carried on is so marginal to evangelical concerns that to bog down in these discussions would mean inevitable neglect of biblical and evangelistic priorities.

Growth of the Bible school movement has been a conspicuous feature of European evangelicalism. Dispensational interests accounted for the early establishment of German schools like the *Bibelmissionsschule* at Beatenberg, an independent venture whose 200 students supply reserves for missionary, pulpit, and evangelistic endeavor as well as for other church work. In Wiedenest the *Bibelmissionshaus,* known beyond its Open Brethren circle through the writings of the late Erich Sauer, has thirty-five students. In Switzerland the *Institut Emmaüs* at Vennes, near Lausanne, with its fifty French-speaking students, has become rather well known through the writings of René Pache; the school has missionary alumni throughout the non-Communist world.

Using the French language and sponsored by four European Bible institutes, a new European seminary has been formed in Paris for students with a baccalaureate diploma; hopefully, it will succeed the seminary at Aix-en-Provence, now slowed almost to a standstill. Cooperating in the project will be the institutes in Brussels (mostly Flemish-speaking), and Nogent-sur-Marne in Paris and Emmaüs in Vennes (both French-speaking). The doctrinal basis includes an unqualified position on the inspiration of the Bible. The faculty is predominantly premillennial.

The most comprehensive Bible school program has been ventured by Greater Europe Mission, whose American leadership was encouraged by Continental evangelicals. (Its field director, Robert Evans, is author of the volume *Let Europe Hear!*) This group now sponsors the European Bible Institute in Lamorlage near Paris (founded in 1952; now has thirty-nine students); *Bibelschule Bergstrasse* in Seeheim, Germany (founded in 1955; has forty-four students); and *Instituto Biblico Evangelico* in Rome (founded in 1960; has graduated its small first class). The objective of Greater Europe Mission is to give nationals who want to enter Christian service a biblical foundation and a sense of evangelistic urgency. From these coeducational institutions the men go out to become assistant pastors in the national churches, pastors of free churches, and evangelists, while the women become youth and children's workers.

DENOMINATIONAL ANXIETIES

In Lutheran and Reformed churches, conservative pastors are increasingly encouraged to sponsor similar study programs on a local church basis to preserve biblical fidelity and promote evangelistic concern. In the people's church, for example, the evangelistic youth work of Wilhelm Busch of Essen, now retired, quickened evangelical sensitivity. Others known for evangelistic initiative and preaching are Hamburg pastor F. Heitmuller, active in the German Evangelistic Alliance; Hans Brandenburg (Lutheran) of Korntal, J. Grünzweig (Moravian Brethren) of Stuttgart, and Heinrich Kemner of Ahlden; Peter Schneider, general secretary of the YMCA, West Berlin; Arno Page of Köln, leader of the Christian Endeavor effort; and Anton Schulte, a free church evangelist who has held community campaigns in Austria and Germany.

Yet no absolute contrast can be drawn between the free churches and the people's (state) church. While the free churches are generally lively and aggressive, individual pastors in the older established denominations have equally vigorous groups. Older pastors in the established churches who reflect the influence of Schlatter, Kähler, or Barth tend to be conservative; the younger generation of ministers has been more largely influenced by Bultmann, an influence increasingly compounded with other emphases as well. The free and people's churches often share similar tendencies. To gain respect or status, many free churches have imitated the state churches organizationally, have become enmeshed in similar theological compromises, have forsaken the proclamation of the Evangel, and have lost their fervor. Yet the people's church goes further amiss by compounding these unfortunate tendencies with public involvement in decisionless Christianity. Because its members are automatically baptized, confirmed, married, and buried by the church, most of them assume that they belong to the Body of Christ irrespective of personal faith. "The churches are state-tax-supported; what other support do they need? And what more do we need than infant baptism and confirmation?" So runs opinion. This lack of spiritual decision in the people's church created a vacuum into which the Bultmannians could readily insert their existential appeal.

In the interest of personal faith both Barth and Brunner have attacked infant baptism; those enrolled in the churches by baptism, they imply, are not on this ground Christians. The baptismal rite has become an increasing problem for Lutheran and Reformed pastors alike. In some places ministers are no longer required to officiate at infant baptism if they have questions of conscience. Some of them encourage the children to wait. Barth has declared for believer's baptism. For some Lutheran theologians this assertion was sufficiently provocative to end any and all interest in his theology. Brunner has hesitated to go this far; the religious structure of Continental civilization is such, he feels, that it cannot stand a renunciation of the validity of infant baptism and confirmation.

7

Reflections on American Theology

WILL PROTESTANT LEADERS in America learn a long overdue lesson from the present theological tumult on the Continent? Will ecumenical synthesizers awake to the meaning of the latest breakdown of European theological perspectives, the third such collapse in the twentieth century? Or will ecclesiastical activism, with its costly forfeiture of intellectual discipline, continue to discourage an independent probing of biblical realities? Will the American religious professionals continue their conformity to the theological fashions set by Continental theorists? Must American divinity students in university-related seminaries and ecumenical centers remain content with dogmatic edifices prefabricated in Europe and simply veneered to denominational preferences by the Methodist introduction of a temperance drydock or the Baptist addition of a pool? Must American theologians under the guise of modernity avidly welcome and perpetuate European religious styles long after the European originals have become outworn and discarded? Has not the time come when the religious professionals might find a summer at home with their Bible more profitable than a few months abroad with the theorists?

In 1957 *Christianity Today* sponsored a theological survey to ascertain the doctrinal convictions of Protestant clergymen in the United States. Opinion Research Corporation of Princeton, New Jersey, conducted a scientific sampling of ministers in all mainline denominations, in the independent fundamentalist churches, and in the so-called third force, excluding only pastors of "store-front" churches.

The survey threw light on the theological situation in America in a remarkable way. It supplied irrefutable evidence that the majority of the Protestant clergy in the United States steadfastly resist the theological dilution of historic Christian convictions that occurs most frequently at the seminary level, and that a wide gap separates the theology of most Protestant ministers from the theological outlook held and promoted by many ecumenical leaders.

To suggest the full significance of the *Christianity Today* survey, some reference must be made to the contemporary theological situation in Europe. Continental religious observers had conceded by 1925, over a generation ago, that "modernism is dead," because the theology of exaggerated divine immanence had been effectively routed by the dialectical-existential theology of radical divine transcendence. From 1925 to 1948 the neo-orthodoxy of Barth and Brunner dominated the European scene with special emphasis on divine wrath and supernatural revelation, and on man's sinfulness and need of miraculous redemption. But by 1950, almost a decade before *Christianity Today*'s American survey, this neo-orthodox thrust was already losing power in Europe. Bultmann and the "demythologizers" arose to refashion dialectical theology; reviving the old liberalism alongside the philosophical notion of *existenz*, existentialism gained ascendancy in many influential theological centers. The miraculous was again dismissed as myth, and the case for Christianity was predicated on the subjectivity of God.

But what was the situation in America during the same period? *Christianity Today*'s 1957 survey, based on a scientific sampling, disclosed several significant and surprising facts about the American theological scene:

1. Of the Protestant clergy, 12 percent designated themselves as theologically "neo-orthodox," 14 percent as theologically "liberal." Hence one in four American Protestant clergymen cherished theological positions that were already discredited and disowned in Europe. (The survey clearly equated liberalism with classic rationalistic modernism and identified neo-orthodoxy with the theology of Barth and Brunner.) Having by-passed conservative theology and presumably championing the cause of modernity, nonevangelical scholars and ministers were in fact propagating theological structures that had already been abandoned abroad. At that time the influence of Bultmann, although rising toward its peak in Europe, was virtually nonexistent in American ministerial circles.

2. Some 74 percent of the Protestant ministers in the United States designated their theology as conservative or fundamentalist. Yet most seminary faculties in the mainstream denominations, denominational leaders in many of the regular churches, and participants in ecumenical dialogue conveyed the impression that evangelical theology was an abandoned option treasured only by a diminishing remnant of uninformed Christians. Liberal–neo-orthodox minorities, depicting themselves as the vanguard of tomorrow, not only penalized evangelical majorities loyal to the historic confessional standards but used ecclesiastical power techniques to drive them underground. Yet almost three out of four ministers rejected the liberal and the neo-orthodox options. A former religion editor of *Time* magazine remarked in 1961 that *Christianity Today* had convinced him that conservative theology is not "simply the parochial viewpoint of Southern Baptists and Missouri Lutherans," and that an international, interdenominational scholarship exists supportive of the evangelical viewpoint.

A number of other conclusions could be drawn on the edge of the 1957 survey. Neo-orthodoxy had gained strength mainly through defections from modernist ranks. There were, indeed, some acquisitions from the fundamentalist side, such as T. F. Torrance of Edinburgh, who swung to Barth, and Dale Moody of Louisville, who swung to Brunner. But these were few when compared with the visible host of deserters moving from humanism and modernism to neo-orthodoxy and not simply to more "realistic" liberalism. (Reinhold Niebuhr's bandwagon seemed to be adding enthusiastic excursionists at almost every liberal waystation.) Yet conservative scholars like E. J. Carnell, P. K. Jewett, Bernard Ramm, S. J. Mikolaski, and others, who exposed themselves to the most persuasive liberal and neo-orthodox scholars, saw no good reason to abandon their evangelical heritage. In Great Britain, scholars like R. V. G. Tasker attested a movement from liberal to conservative positions, while on the Continent churchmen like Pierre Corthiel of Paris gave evidence of a movement from neo-orthodox to evangelical ground.

Although from Edwin Lewis to William Hordern the [neo-orthodox] movement's spokesmen trumpeted neo-orthodoxy as America's faith of the future, it failed to gather into its fold fully half of the clergy that were nonevangelical.

Hordern himself was never fully comfortable in the neo-orthodox climate; in respect to revelation and reason and revelation and history he veered toward evangelical positions. Dialectical theology devalued reason and history, and this as much as its revival of miraculous supernaturalism dimmed the interest of American liberals. With the passing of the years, *Christianity*

Today's survey gained greater significance for its disclosure that, even at the high tide of American enthusiasm for the Barth-Brunner theology, liberal clergy (14 percent) still outnumbered neo-orthodox clergy (12 percent). In the United States liberal Protestants considered neo-orthodoxy not so much a theological alternative as a challenge to self-correction. The ranks of the "chastened" liberals multiplied as historical events forced a revision of the prevailing optimistic views of man. But these liberal "realists" refused to move to neo-orthodox perspectives. Their leaders included Reinhold Niebuhr, Robert C. Calhoun, Paul Tillich, H. Richard Niebuhr, Walter Marshall Horton, John C. Bennett, H. Shelton Smith, and L. Harold DeWolf. Among the barriers to their acceptance of neo-orthodoxy were Barth's miraculous supernaturalism (the Virgin Birth), his insistence on the absolute uniqueness and singularity of divine revelation, and his consequent rejecton of philosophical apologetics. Brunner with his emphasis on general revelation gained a wider hearing. In contrast to Scotland, where dialectical theology and then existentialism found the door quite open, the reaction to Continental dogmatics was substantially the same in England as in America.

The regrouping liberal forces in America have remained almost fatally divided. While there is now more talk of neo-liberalism than of neo-orthodoxy, the lines of distinction are found in the rejection of objectionable positions rather than in the systematic formulation of a consistent and coherent dogmatics. Signs of a merger of Tillich's thought with Bultmann's are regarded as further evidence of decline in the influence of both viewpoints. On the one hand, neo-liberals are "in search of a system"; on the other hand, their underlying commitment to a methodology of tentativity poses an obstacle to any monogamous marriage. The perpetual liberal revision of theological affirmations has bred disillusionment and disinterest in the realm of doctrine, or simply a pragmatic nonchalance. There seems no bright prospect among liberals of a unifying theological leadership. The two rallying cries of the Protestant liberals are ecumenism (the outward visible unity of Christendom) and American political liberalism (the implementation of socio-economic changes by legislative programs). Many spokesmen simply substitute a lively conscience on the race question for any recognizable theology.

If the American neo-liberals would meditate on the drift of recent European thought, they would realize why Continental scholars, unimpressed by any such narrow theological framework, have already bypassed neo-liberal dogmatic positions either on the way up or on the way down. Whoever renounces the reality of an external criterion of theological truth cannot claim to take divine revelation seriously, and whoever locates the essence of revealed religion in subjective awareness must disown the religion of the Bible.

Meanwhile there can be little doubt of a resurgence of evangelical theology. All estimations of this renewal as merely an "undertow," or a marginal backlash of sorts, fail to do justice to its creative initiative and forward movement. Although its gains are sometimes attributed almost wholly to independent fundamentalist circles outside the ecumenical movement, the facts are otherwise. The systematic elimination of dynamic conservative theological centers by ecumenically minded denominations and the transformation of these centers into theologically inclusive institutions has doubtless tended to repress evangelical strength among more recent graduates; but it has also failed to produce articulate disciples for an alternative point of view. Assuredly, there appears no great hope for a spectacular shift to the right in the seminaries of world ecumenical renown. Yet the evangelical resurgence is no secondary current to be contrasted with the mainstream itself. There are many articulate evangelical spokesmen in mainstream Christianity. In a number of old-line denominations most of the clergy are still theologically evangelical, even though they are not proportionately represented in denominational or ecumenical leadership.

In England this evangelical renewal is evident not only from the enlarging interest in the Puritan writings but also from the noteworthy increase of meritorious conservative literature by contemporary writers. In America also evangelical writers have steadily expanded their theological contribution. The Evangelical Book Club now has 20,000 members; some solid conservative works have gone into 40,000 or more ministerial and lay homes; and the number of competent young evangelical scholars sharing the task of creative literary effort is growing. No definitive work in systematic theology has recently appeared either in Britain or in the United States comparable to G. C. Berkouwer's *Studies in Dogmatics* in the Netherlands. Yet the two-volume *A Systematic Theology of the Christian Religion by* J. Oliver Buswell, Jr. (Zondervan, 1963), is the most recent in a succession of evangelical efforts in America that recognize that any theology worthy of biblical Christianity must do full justice to scriptural claims. *Christianity Today,* moreover, has served as a fulcrum of contemporary evangelical conviction and as a rallying point for the conservative cause. The evangelical resurgence, therefore, is by no means confined to Billy Graham's phenomenal inroads at the evangelistic frontier; it also affects contemporary religious thought.

Some Protestant circles today are increasingly troubled over the virtual loss in ecumenical circles of any sense of the unique importance of the canon of scriptural writings. In contrast to the nonevangelical indifference to the Bible as the only authoritative norm of faith and practice, evangelicals champion the authority and plenary inspiration of the Scriptures. They are keenly aware that Christian theology requires a doctrine of the Word of God that is lost to liberal theology, and a better doctrine of the Word of God than Barth and Brunner offer. Conservative theology has faced tensions of its own about the doctrine of Scripture, and not all the questions and doubts are resolved. Among conservatives the main point of contention is the inerrancy or infallibility of Scripture, a question that has recently vexed a number of institutions. Some evangelical scholars have long debated whether affirmation of the Bible as "the only infallible rule of faith and practice" embraces historical and scientific facets also, or whether scriptural reliability in the latter area is inconsequential. In Britain, theistic evolution and immanental theology influenced the evangelical mainstream late in the nineteenth century, and stalwarts like James Orr yielded ground in the area of full biblical authority. In America, the Princeton scholars Hodge and Warfield stressed that a theory of Christian knowledge built on such compromise could not stand. Warfield's work on *The Inspiration and Authority of the Bible* is still relevant reading; the chapter on "The Real Problem of Inspiration" has never been effectively answered.

Christianity Today's 1957 survey indicated that of the evangelical 74 percent of American ministerial ranks, 35 percent preferred to be designated as fundamentalist and 39 percent as conservative. The survey distinguished these two groups on the question of biblical inerrancy. Fundamentalists subscribe to inerrancy, but conservatives have some reservations about it. One interesting development on the American scene was the founding in 1950 of the Evangelical Theological Society, which is composed of scholars who profess adherence to an inerrant Scripture. There are now some 400 members. Although the society has sponsored publication of a number of worthy projects, the membership's literary productivity is hardly proportionate to its numerical strength. But the society does provide a cohesive theological stimulus lacking among other evangelical scholars who have reservations about the high view of the Bible.

One reason for the stratification of American theology is the lack of communication between divergent schools of thought. Ecumenical and denominational dialogue has tended to crowd out evangelical participation. In some denominations evangelical and nonevangelical theologians seem to converse only at annual interseminary banquets. Most evangelical scholars are now concentrated in independent or interdenominational institutions, since the ecumenical emphasis tends to generate theologically inclusive faculties in denominational life. For two generations nonevangelical theologians in America have dismissed their evangelical counterparts as nothing but dogmatic purveyors of a dispensable tradition while they themselves have dispensed alternatives imported from Europe. These alternatives, however, often had already been abandoned abroad while their American sponsors were busy extolling their enduring merit. The American seminary scene would benefit from creative dialogue predicated on a realistic assessment of the lamentable dearth of enduring theology. It is high time theologians who profess to be on special terms with Deity begin conversations across theological lines.

THEOLOGICAL DEFAULT IN SEMINARIES

The wave of Bultmannian teaching and writing now flooding American seminaries is a sorry commentary on religious thought in this country. Not only does it attest the lack of independent theological virility in America, a fact lamentable in itself; it also repeats the costly tendency to popularize speculative notions already discredited abroad. Before World War II, liberal theologians in America were indoctrinating seminary students with a theology supposedly as up-to-date as to-morrow (the modernism these young professors had absorbed in their doctoral studies abroad). But in the meantime classic modernism was already being dis-carded in Europe as outworn and untrue. Then the American "frontiersmen" moved toward crisis-theology, and by 1958 almost as many Protestant ministers listed themselves in the neo-orthodox camp as in the modern-ist movement. Barth and Brunner were the luminaries of these Americans, and little mention was being made of Bultmann. Barth and Brunner, however, were soon to acknowledge Bultmann's command of the theological dialogue. And now that the Bultmannian empire is breaking up in Europe, the American Protestant semi-naries are predictably becoming a Johnny-come-lately Bultmannian circuit.

Amid the professorial cross fire and combat on Conti-nental seminary campuses, most European students are withholding any personal commitment to Bultmann's theology. They learn Bultmann's position, yes, but fly no Bultmannian banners. As George Traar, superin-tendent for the Evangelical (Lutheran) Church for Vienna, puts it, students are equally interested in "what others are saying—not only Bultmannians, but anti-Bultmannians." "Bultmann's solutions are bypassed and his methodology of existential interpretation is under such fire," says Helmut Thielicke of Hamburg, "that students no longer are transfixed by the claims of the Bultmann scholars, and their minds are open to a hearing for alternative viewpoints."

"The German students like the ancient Athenians are

especially on the lookout for novel points of view," remarks another Continental theologian. "That is why our textbooks live only for a couple of years. Students are interested in watching a fight—in hearing theologians who make cutting remarks about competitors and colleagues; scholarship and relevance and dialogue no longer seem to assure an atmosphere of enthusiasm. The younger generation now seems more disposed to watch the theological controversy than to join it."

In America things are worse. Seminary students are content with European leftovers specially seasoned by American dieticians against decomposition.

Despite the decline of Bultmann's prestige and influence in Europe, and just at the time when Continental scholars and students are veering from a commitment to his views, American divinity students abroad and some seminary professors in the States are rallying to "modern" perspectives already considered dated and doomed on the European side. The latest theological fashions in America have traditionally lagged a half generation or more behind European influences. Subsequently this European inheritance has been carried to radical extremes, long after its underlying presuppositions were abandoned abroad. There are numerous indications that this unpromising process may now be repeated once again.

No wholesale exportation of Bultmannism to the United States is likely, it should be noted, for the simple reason that American philosophy does not contain the background of existentialism which this theology presupposes. Where no background of existential philosophy exists, the Bultmannian insistence that Christianity must be translated into existential categories to become relevant and intelligible to the modern man becomes nonsense. This dissimilar philosophical background is one explanation for the difficulty of negotiating effective American-European theological dialogue on the frontiers of contemporary religious thought.

Yet an *avant-garde* minority is energetically carrying Bultmann's theology to the American scene. And through its influence upon ministerial students in the seminaries, the Bultmannian speculation sooner or later will be felt in certain church-related colleges and in the churches themselves. American graduate students abroad, always open to new idols and finding none at home during liberalism's present transition period, are committing themselves to Bultmannian positions in conspicuously greater numbers than are Continental scholars. At the Montreal Faith and Order Conference in 1963 it became clear that World Council programming hoped to give Bultmann scholars a larger role in the theological dialogue. American seminaries have welcomed an increasing Bultmannian exposure. Bornkamm and Conzelmann have given lectures here in the past; Käsemann visited Yale and San Anselmo in 1965. At Drew, Union, Claremont, and Harvard, Bultmannian scholars have served or are now serving as professors. Macmillan will soon publish its volume on Bultmann in the Kegley and Bretall "Living Theologians" series, and denominational as well as secular publishing houses have increased the tempo of Bultmann-oriented religious books. Volumes one and two in the Harper and Row series devoted to European-American dialogue on major theological issues, cited by James M. Robinson and John B. Cobb of Southern California School of Theology, are given over to existentialist concerns. Both books, *The Later Heidegger and Theology* and *The New Hermeneutic,* are so heavy and abstruse as virtually to nullify a similar complaint by one of the contributors against German theologians! Yet those who peruse the recent volume entitled *The Historical Jesus and the Kerygmatic Christ* (Carl E.

Braaten and Roy A. Harrisville, editors, Abingdon, 1964), with its essay on this central point of contemporary theological debate, will find the complaint amply justified. Not all the volumes on the margin of the Bultmannian controversy settle for Bultmannian or post-Bultmannian positions. Some, like Hugh Anderson's *Jesus and Christian Origins* (Oxford, 1964), deplore the new quest's correlation of historical inquiry with a special brand of philosophical speculation. Anderson demands a larger role for the historical ingredient in Christianity, yet gives half his case away to the demythologizers. Some of the new works are basic theological tools. But none says openly what needs to be said—that contemporary Protestant theologians are largely lost in wildernesses of speculation, and that further progress can now be made in theology only by asking not where Barth, Brunner, and Bultmann end but where the Bible begins.

Despite the absence of a native American tradition of existential philosophy, other factors contribute a mood compatible with Bultmannian views. The American theological interest in Kierkegaard and in Barth and Brunner as well as in Bultmann has encouraged religious interest in both dialectical and existential premises. Much of American liberalism had already shared neo-orthodoxy's skepticism over the ontological significance of reason; that is, over the rational structure of the metaphysical world and the competence of human reason to understand spiritual realities. Further, the trend toward analytic philosophy and linguistic analysis has tended to limit the search for universally valid meaning to the world of sense realities. The most influential theological figures in America, Reinhold Niebuhr and Paul Tillich, themselves have emphasized that reason can expound the supernatural realm only in symbolic or figurative categories.

Despite its pursuit of the latest fashions in European thought, the theology in American seminaries is touching mainly the formative principles that distinguish Bultmannian from non-Bultmannian positions. Whereas European scholars reflect a mood that runs increasingly contrary to Bultmann, American religious speculation at the frontiers reflects much more Bultmannian sympathy. In their studies of the Bultmann tradition, American graduate students abroad scarcely have time to keep up with the most recent books. Many volumes are increasingly critical of Bultmannism; many are not yet translated, and some undoubtedly never will be. It is strange, indeed, that pulpits of university churches and teaching posts in church-related colleges as well as in seminaries so often are reserved for doctorate-holding scholars who return to America as flag-wavers for European systems, especially when abroad these systems are already outmoded and in disrepute.

In view of the breakup of Bultmannian positions, Werner Georg Kümmel of Marburg, ex-president of the Society of New Testament Studies, cannot understand why "the younger grandsons of Bultmann keep getting chair after chair in the theological seminaries." "The post-Bultmannians continue to get the spoils," he comments, "although the unity of the Bultmann school is shattered."

Many seminaries have become so much the purveyors of abstruse theological speculations, and give so little evidence of a fixed authoritative norm, that they seem to be making themselves theologically dispensable. Contemporary theologizing has become an exceedingly perishable commodity. Doubtless some seminaries remain denominationally or ecumenically indispensable for ecclesiastical objectives. But in a warring age at the brink of self-destruction, when scientists think that 22,300 miles out in space is no place for mistakes, one might wish that the seminaries on terra firma would forego the business of propagating heresy generation upon generation.

It is as true in America as in Europe that on university campuses the theologians are today looked upon as an inferior academic species. Claiming a private pipeline to the supernatural, they refashion their gods every generation. And American theologians are notoriously predictable. Unless they stand in the mainstream of evangelical Christianity, committed to the God of Moses, Isaiah, and Paul, they are forever resurrecting the ghosts of recently buried European dogmatic speculation. The theologians can hardly be fully blamed— they are student-victims of earlier theologians addicted to the same error. And each generation of students seems to drink from the same bitter wells.

EVANGELICALS AND DIALOGUE

A survey of the membership of the Evangelical Theological Society discloses that many conservative scholars concentrate their interest upon a few lively concerns, and that wide gaps exist in evangelical research.

From the responses of 112 members *Christianity Today* has learned that two out of three evangelical scholars think biblical authority is the main theological theme now under review in conservative circles in America. Of these scholars, more than half trace this development to pressures for doctrinal redefinition resulting from recent theological speculations about the nature of divine revelation.

One in three conservative scholars singles out ecclesiology, or the doctrine of the Church, as the critical area in contemporary theological study. Eschatology (the doctrine of the end-time) and the nature of God were listed as other priority concerns. The respondents put soteriology, the saving work of Christ, in fifth place, and the doctrine of sanctification in sixth place, as theological areas under special pressure for critical modification.

The compromise of the authority of the Bible noticeable in many mainstream Protestant denominations is viewed as a lamentable surrender of scriptural perspectives to modern critical speculations. The result of the critical assaults has been to qualify the historic Christian view of the Bible by multiplying doubts over historical and propositional revelation, plenary inspiration, and verbal inerrancy.

The evangelical reply to this critical trend, the survey discloses, is not one of simple and naïve negation. Since the Bible is a mooring that holds Protestant Christianity from drifting aimlessly on a wide sea of subjective speculation, the case for scriptural authority calls for clear exposition. The conservative emphasis on divine revelation and on the deeds of God as the foundation of Christian faith is studied and positive.

Yet the replies confirm the judgment that affirmations of the high view of Scripture in the catalogues of evangelical seminaries, colleges, and Bible institutes do not reflect the extent to which some faculties are struggling with the issue of reaffirmation or redefinition. A plea is widely sounded for interpreting the Bible "in the light of its revelational purpose." At times this formula is taken simply as a warning against seeking scriptural solutions to questions that the sacred writers never intended to answer (for example, the effect of chemicals on moral decisions). Sometimes its implications are broader, so that the reliability of Scripture is limited to doctrinal and moral elements at the expense of historical and scientific content, the net result of which is a refusal to view the Bible as a document of unbroken divine authority.

Emphasis on divine confrontation and human encounter tends to weaken some expositions of a completed past revelation, and to give a neo-evangelical and almost neo-orthodox character to subjective-experiential factors at the expense of objective orthodoxy. Doctoral dissertations written by some conservative American scholars under neo-orthodox teachers at Edinburgh, Basel, Princeton, and Drew attest this conformity to present theological pressures. Instead of trying to justify this existential emphasis on the basis of Luther and Calvin, however, these neo-conservatives criticize the early Reformers as well as their more recent exponents, Charles Hodge and B. B. Warfield in particular. A noteworthy feature of this neo-conservative negation is that it has not issued in any consistent or stable alternative to the position it criticizes; in this respect it is a theology with a fluid notion of religious authority and is particularly vulnerable to considerable further pressure.

Yet even in these circles there remains the recognition that without the authority of Scripture Protestantism too may soon become merely an echo of a decadent society. All evangelical scholars repudiate the reduction of *"thus saith the Lord"* to "it seems to me." They deplore "demythologizing" as only a modern revival of unbelief of an ancient gnostic type. They abhor radical philosophical postures. They reject the far-out theories that religious concepts are only symbolic and not normative or informative, and that theological language has no fixed or absolute significance. They reject the existential view of revelation as mere subjective act or event. While they seek rapprochement with modern science, they are wholly undisposed to rule out the miraculous, to subordinate divine factors to human, or to locate the center of religious authority in man's experience and thus to substitute a rationalistic for a revelational understanding of the supernatural.

In evangelical circles the tension over the Bible does not spring from a desire to accommodate Christian realities to a secular world view. In the question of how God acts in nature and history the character and words of God are seen to be at stake. If He does not act in the way the Bible says (or "means"), the result is a different religion from historic Christianity. Many significant expositions of the Protestant position still view Calvin's *Institutes* as a major contribution to the doctrine of Scripture as revelation.

Nonetheless tension arises in evangelical circles through the inordinate pressures of contemporary scientific theory about the antiquity of man. Christian anthropologists are by no means agreed on an interpretation of the data, but those who insist that *homo sapiens* is hundreds of thousands of years old make little effort to correlate this conclusion with an insistence on objective historical factuality in respect to the fall of the first man, Adam, and its implications for the entire human race. Among many evangelical biblical scholars, moreover, one can discern an assignment of priority to salvation-history over revealed truth. Thus an emphasis on the God who acts and on his concrete historical revelation tends to replace that on *the God who speaks and acts;* interest in a dynamic deity acting in history comes to supplant interest in verbal inspiration. The Bible may survive as a religious document through which God still speaks uniquely, but it no longer is assigned objective authority in the classical Protestant sense, for the unchanging factual character of revealed truth is in doubt. The most recent effort in this twilight zone, Dewey Beegle's book on *The Inspiration of Scripture,* satisfied neither conservative, neo-orthodox, nor liberal critics, since it blended elements from all three positions. Beegle later protested that the publishers

(Westminster Press) had deleted important evangelical sections of the volume.

Debate over the Bible seems again to be hardening into a "party struggle" over the nature of revelation and authority. Liberal, neo-orthodox, and conservative scholars now all appeal to a "Word of God," but they do not mean the same thing. Liberalism balks at objective authority and pole-vaults over the miracles of the Christian religion; neo-orthodoxy hedges over revealed information and plays leap-frog with the miraculous. Neo-orthodoxy discusses revelation in God's "acts" from the vantage point of psychology of religion alongside an oral tradition and source-theory of Scripture. Every evangelical effort to bridge the gap to nonevangelical scholars ends up with an impossible demand for the surrender of verbal and plenary inspiration and propositional revelation as well.

Evangelical scholars are fully aware that the doctrine of the Bible controls all other doctrines of the Christian faith. "A correct view of the Bible (its inspiration, nature, and authority)," insists one theologian, "is prior in importance to any other doctrine." "Dilute or dismiss the authority of the Bible and other doctrinal matters will not long remain in the center of discussion," comments a New Testament professor, "since no authoritative voice remains to decide what they shall be." Another scholar comments: "The doctrine of Scripture is fundamental to all others. The source of knowledge governs the results. Even the doctrine of Christ and salvation depends on it." "Without an authoritative Bible," remarks another, "even the authority of Jesus Christ is eroded; deep down all the major problems involve the question of biblical authority, for it affects all the realms of doctrine and life, including the life and witness of the Church." And another spokesman puts it thus: "The formal principle of Protestantism is the objective and sole authority of the Bible. The material principle is salvation by grace alone. Both are undermined by the view of the Bible which is becoming dominant today."

It is noteworthy that no contemporary Protestant theologian has dealt exhaustively with the subject of biblical authority in the context of the broadest ecumenical dialogue. Evangelical discussion often concentrates on objections to the conservative view, or on rear-guard controversies within the conservative camp, to the neglect of a comprehensive statement of its own position. The evangelical critique is oriented to liberal and neo-orthodox deviations, and it is ill-prepared for dialogue with Roman Catholicism at a time when Rome is assigning new scope to the Bible and restudying its own view of church authority. Meanwhile a growing role for church authority in ecumenical circles, along with an unsure position on the role of the Scripture, leaves the ecumenical dialogue open and vulnerable to both Eastern Orthodox and Roman Catholic counterclaims. Everyman perforce will have some authority—if not the Bible or the Church, then his own reason, tradition, or "experience." The ecumenical Protestant loss of an authoritative Bible has shaped a vacuum which, for a time, is likely to be filled by ecclesiastical commitments but which ultimately could be filled simply by church decree, whether post-Protestant or Roman Catholic.

Evangelicals do not dispute the fact that for a time at least Christianity may function with an impaired doctrine of Scripture. But it does so at its own peril and inevitably must then lose much of its essential message. The strength of the evangelical view has been demonstrated in manifold ways in the aftermath of the liberal erosion of Christian authority. Evangelist Billy Graham's emphasis on what "the Bible says" attests the enduring grip of scriptural revelation on needy human hearts. The Christian colleges graduate a steady stream of ministers and missionaries whose doctrinal stability is evident in a time of theological flux, and send an expanding task force of devout laymen into the metropolitan and rural areas of American life. The Evangelical Theological Society promotes scholarly inquiry premised on the full authority of Scripture and provides association and fellowship for scholars convinced of the inadequacy of nonevangelical views. The superiority of the conservative view has been effectively argued in many volumes. The literature includes such symposiums as *Revelation and the Bible* (Carl F. H. Henry, ed.), *The Infallible Word* (N. B. Stonehouse and Paul Woolley, eds.), and *Inspiration and Interpretation* (John F. Walvoord, ed.). Noteworthy volumes are J. I. Packer, *Fundamentalism and the Word of God;* Bernard Ramm, *Special Revelation and the Word of God;* Edward J. Young, *The Word of Truth;* Wick Broomall, *Biblical Criticism.* Related contributions include G. C. Berkouwer's *The Triumph of Grace in the Theology of Karl Barth,* Gordon H. Clark's *Karl Barth's Theological Method* and *Reason, Religion and Revelation,* Paul K. Jewett's *Emil Brunner's Concept of Revelation,* and Cornelius Van Til's *Christianity and Barthianism.* The appearance of *The Holman Study Bible* and *The Harper Study Bible* attests the continuing interest in Scripture study by readers holding a high view of the Bible.

If the strength of American evangelicalism rests in its high view of Scripture, its weakness lies in a tendency to neglect the frontiers of formative discussion in contemporary theology. Thus evangelicals forfeit the debate at these points to proponents of subevangelical points of view, or to those who assert evangelical positions in only a fragmentary way. One can understand why it is necessary to emphasize continually that the best precaution against burning down the house of faith is not to play with incendiary criticism. But when the edifice is already afire, the extinguisher needs to be concentrated immediately and directly on the consuming sweep of the flames.

The element missing in much evangelical theological writing is an air of exciting relevance. The problem is not that biblical theology is outdated; it is rather that some of its expositors seem out of touch with the frontiers of doubt in our day. Theology textbooks a half century old sometimes offer more solid content than the more recent tracts-for-the-times, but it is to the credit of some contemporary theologians that they preserve a spirit of theological excitement and fresh relevance. Evangelicals need to overcome any impression that they are merely retooling the past and repeating clichés. If Bible reading has undergone a revolution through the preparation of new translations in the idiom of the decade, the theology classroom in many conservative institutions needs to expound the enduring truths in the setting and language of the times. Unless we speak to our generation in a compelling idiom, meshing the great theological concerns with current modes of thought and critical problems of the day, we shall speak only to ourselves.

Almost every evangelical scholar, moreover, voices some complaint about the present theological situation, but only a minority share in the burdens of conservative scholarship and contribute concretely to an evangelical alternative. There is presently no better framework than the Evangelical Theological Society to enlist conservative resources in a coordinated theological offensive, although the society has not as yet effectively marshalled its forces.

Specific areas of theological concern meanwhile press

for evangelical attention. A comprehensive statement of evangelical theology from American sources, comparable to Berkouwer's *Studies in Dogmatics* in The Netherlands, remains a necessary project. To serve its purpose, such an effort must give attention to the theological frontiers of special interest to the contemporary religious dialogue. The great issues of authority, revelation, history, the canon, and ecumenism call for sustained study. There must be room also for specialized studies that may not seem particularly relevant to present developments at the frontiers of current religious thought, in view of the fact that theologians converse over mobile fences. But contemporary Christianity is face-to-face with a major transition time in theology, and this affords evangelicals a providential moment for earnest engagement.

Just now the theological debate has moved closer to central evangelical concerns than it had for several decades. In the current controversy over the connection of revelation and history, and of revelation and truth, American evangelicals have a strategic opportunity to contribute at the moving frontier of contemporary theological dialogue.

8

Modern Theology
at the End of Its Tether

A SPATE OF BOOKS and articles is currently appearing on "the problem of God," assuring us, in the name of the modern intellectual, that God is indeed an enigma to the man of our times. Sophisticated interpreters of the latest mood tell us that the crucial issue is how to present Christianity intelligibly to the modern mind in order to overcome "the God-problem" in present-day society. The alien cultural setting of the late twentieth century, we are told, demands a "contemporary understanding" of the Gospel because of the special stance of the "godless" man of our times. In certain seminary classrooms and in the writings of certain churchmen, one now finds supposedly serious proponents of the Christian religion assuring us that mankind has outgrown an adolescent religious stage wherein God was viewed as transcendent personality providing supernatural salvation, and that the human race is now too adult to take the theology of the Bible literally.

Anybody familiar with the history of philosophy will recognize this so-called gospel of modernity as antique rationalism. Hardcore naturalists have made essentially the same claim of up-to-dateness whenever they have aimed their propaganda attack against the reality of the supernatural, against the essential uniqueness of man, and against the changeless character of truth and the good. What is new in this recent turn is (1) that some widely publicized theologians and churchmen are saying it; (2) that they are saying it not after openly forsaking the Church for the world but rather within the Church itself; and (3) that at the same time they are welcomed as authentic Christian voices in denominational and ecumenical dialogue. Although ecclesiastical spokesmen who thus sift ultimate reality through the sieve of empirico-scientific categories are not in every case prominent or spectacular, nevertheless a surprising number hold seminary teaching posts and profess devotion to the New Testament.

These theological faddists reject the right of revealed religion to disclose how reality is objectively constituted and proceed to construct an antimetaphysical or non-metaphysical "Christianity." The way for an acceptance of their views was unfortunately, and sometimes unwittingly, prepared by the whole movement of recent modern religious thought from Kant to Kierkegaard to Bultmann. Although the dialectical and existential theologians reasserted the reality of the transcendent and insisted on special divine revelation, these theologians were anti-intellectualistic in the sense that they denied the ability of conceptual reason, even on the basis of revelation, to acquire objective and universally valid knowledge of transcendent Being. The net effect of this entire movement of religious thought was to undermine confidence in orthodox Protestant theology as an authentic exposition of supernatural realities.

In the post-World War I ferment, Rudolf Bultmann made a spectacular effort to conform Christianity to the modern scientific world view. His existential theology insisted on the reality of the transcendent but spoke of the supernatural as myth. The biblical account of the supernatural, the Bultmannians contend, aims to promote our self-understanding and need of spiritual decision, not to give us objective truth about God or to inform us how ultimate reality is constituted. Bultmann's emphasis on existential self-understanding was aimed to forestall the empirico-scientific reduction of man to abstract, impersonal categories neglectful of the volitional, emotional, and subconscious aspects of his experience. Bultmann minimized the importance of the historical aspects of Jesus' life as unimportant for faith and stressed the centrality of the kerygma—the apostolic preaching of Jesus Christ. For almost a decade this existential reduction of the Gospel became the rallying cry of young intellectuals in German seminaries. But supporters of this pseudo-Christian ideology have split into rival camps, and its foundations are now so widely viewed as tottering that most religious frontiersmen are consciously seeking an alternative. The Bultmannian forces are decimated but not wholly demolished; the movement lives on in "the new hermeneutic" sparked by Fuchs and Ebeling in Germany and by Robinson and Michalson in America; and Conzelmann, Dinkler, and even Käsemann retain significant loyalties to the dethroned monarch of Marburg existentialism. But the Bultmannians have ascribed to the Bible positions and meanings the New Testament does not validate. The New Testament Gospel includes the total public ministry of Jesus Christ; Mark's account opens with the declaration that Jesus' baptism is the beginning of the Gospel, even as the resurrection is the climax. Moreover, the New Testament includes affirmations about the transcendent nature of God and the historical character of his acts.

LINGUISTIC THEOLOGY

Ever since Karl Barth and Emil Brunner exposed classic modernism as a rationalistic heresy, many British and American liberals have been eager to fly a new flag. In recent generations, American liberals promptly appropriated the main motifs of German speculation, and extremists readily carried these tenets to radical positions. The breakdown of Barth's influence, however, and the evident decline and decay of Bultmannian theology have herded American liberals of antimetaphysical temperament into the expanding fold of analytical philosophy as a refuge from historic Christian faith. Analytical philosophers regard the function of philosophy neither as the construction of a metaphysical theory embracing ultimate reality nor as the provision of answers to persistent questions about man and the world, but as the clarification of all assertions. Analysis of concepts has always been an essential preliminary task of philosophy, but linguistic analysis is now asserted to be its main, even its exclusive, function, with a view not to the discovery of fact or the determination of truth but to the clarification of meaning.

After A. J. Ayer's *Language, Truth and Logic* (London: V. Gollancz, 1936) lifted logical positivism to prominence beyond the attention commanded by such earlier proponents of analytic philosophy as G. E. Moore and Bertrand Russell, empirical verifiability gained acceptance as the criterion of meaning. The patent fact that metaphysical, theological, and ethical statements are empirically unverifiable came to signal a radical assault on the truth-character of religious assertions.

Such theological innovators now find the secret of "up-to-the-minute" accommodation of Christianity to "empirico-scientific reality," in a speculative view of "the function of religious language," not in mythical interpretation of the Bible alongside an existential philosophy of self-understanding. Contemporary linguistic analysis becomes the open-sesame of religious intelligibility and acceptability. The inner spirit of the present age is arbitrarily equated with the prejudices of the analytic philosophy, which requires any and all reality to register its presence on the radar screen of empirico-scientific method. Whereas the Bultmannians built on the pervasive academic influence of Heidegger's existentialism, and in this context sought to vindicate a permanent role for Christianity by existentializing the New Testament message, the "linguistic theologians" seek to vindicate religion in the current climate of analytic philosophy by secularizing Christianity. To authenticate religious experience on this universal basis, the linguistic theologians dismiss even Bultmann's attenuated interest in the kerygma of Jesus Christ.

While the linguistic theologians, over against the logical positivists, deplore the restriction of meaning to empirically verifiable statements, they nonetheless defend the validity of religious language on other grounds than truth. The value of traditional religious affirmation is not preserved as conceptually significant; instead, the verificational analysis is functional. Ludwig Wittgenstein's insistence on a variety of "language-games" has encouraged some analysts to defend religious affirmations as "meaningful assertions of relationships" not empirically verifiable. Religious beliefs are assigned therapeutic significance, or are viewed as meeting a psychological necessity in human life, or as providing experience with creative human models akin to working models in the scientific world. Such validation of religious belief nowhere answers the modern mind's insistent question whether or not religious beliefs are *true,* not simply useful or helpful.

If the realm of cognitive language must be denuded of all transempirical concepts, then no affirmations about the supernatural are rationally verifiable, and no reason can any longer be given for preferring one metaphysics or ontology above another, nor for regarding any view of ultimate reality as right. If all religious concepts are banished beyond the realm of verification —and remain outside the arena of truth or falsehood— no reason can be adduced for choosing one faith or set of religious beliefs over its opposite, or, for that matter, for choosing any at all on rational grounds. But regardless of the piety, prominence, or presumption of theologians who insist merely that religious views are pragmatically or psychologically serviceable, twentieth-century men can be counted on swiftly to abandon beliefs they can no longer cherish as true.

DEATH OF GOD THEOLOGY

Among some theologians, the empirical validation of Christianity leads not to a special role for religious language as much as to a deliberate restatement of Christianity and of the Gospel in secular this-worldly terms. The secular theologians all reject objective ontological and dogmatic language about a transcendent Deity, and they extend the revolt against an intelligible revelation of the Transcendent so as to include within the category of myth even the kerygmatic elements on which recent European theology has insisted.

Secular theology is postexistentialist and post-European in that it summons contemporary Protestant theologians to end their "crying out to God." Theological language is tapered to statements about Jesus of Nazareth and human self-understanding, contrary to Bultmann's displacement of the historical basis of faith by the notion of authentic existence, and contrary also to the discovery by linguistic theologians of the "special" significance of universal religious affirmations. These secular theologians are not concerned simply because supersensible realities are without effective force in modern life; they boldly aim to make religion relevant by erasing its supernatural aspects entirely. If the dialectical and existential theologies turned aside from "objectified theism" and viewed existence as an inappropriate term when speaking of God, the secular theologians now reject "nonobjectified theism" as well. From the objective-transcendent personal God of Judeo-Christian theology, therefore, neo-Protestant interpreters have moved in recent generations to the nonobjective-transcendent personal God (Barth and Brunner), to the nonobjective-transcendent impersonal Unconditioned (Tillich), to the nonobjective-mythological-transcendent personal God (Bultmann), to nonobjective-nontranscendent religion. Thomas J. J. Altizer views "the death of God" as a "historical event" datable in our own lifetime, and offers his religious speculations as an example of relevant theologizing in the time of "the death of God." Paul M. van Buren obligingly informs us that "the word 'God' is dead."[1] What remains is the man Jesus—his life and death and availability for others, his values, and the contagion of his perspective, urging us to freedom from self-concern and to self-surrender for others. But skillful critics observe that, on the one hand, Van Buren's "secularized Christianity" perverts the essence of New Testament Christianity no less than does Bultmann's existentialism, and that, on the other hand, by championing the ethical centrality of Jesus as one who calls us to serve in the world, "secularized Christianity" espouses a selection of values fully as unintelligible and offensive to the modern empirico-scientific outlook as the traditional concepts Van Buren proposes to replace.

On the assumption that modern knowledge renders unintelligible the scriptural formulation of the Gospel, the secular theologians eliminate the invisible, transcendent, absolute God of the Bible. Christianity must,

---

[1]Paul M. van Buren, *The Secular Meaning of the Gospel* (New York: The Macmillan Co., 1963), p. 103.

we are told, dispense wholly with "God-talk" in order to become relevant, appropriate, and intelligible to the man of the late 1960s. All references to the supernatural God, to supernatural relationships, even to dependence on the supernatural, are spurned; and in consequence of this distrust of the suprahistorical and supernatural, the transempirical is translated into the empirical. The metaphysical and cosmological aspects of revealed religion are thereby eliminated and the relevant subject matter of theology reduced to the historical, human, and ethical.

If this maneuver were ventured frankly as an open and avowed repudiation of revealed religion, confusion would be lessened and truth and fact advanced, since God and Christ and redemption and the Church lose their biblical actuality in these contemporary fabrications. But Bishop John Robinson promulgates his *Honest to God* as an authentic revised version of biblical Christianity, while Van Buren seeks to assure us that his secularized Christianity omits "nothing essential" to Christian faith. Yet these and similar efforts—among them William Hamilton's *The New Essence of Christianity* (Association Press, 1961) and Altizer's *Mircea Eliade and the Dialectic of the Sacred* (Westminster, 1963)—not only violate the essential spirit and substance of historic Christianity but radically alter the role of religion in human life.

MISUNDERSTANDING OF MAN

The most obvious defect of this contemporary theological faddism is its mislocation of the problem of modern man. Whether modern man's special difficulty is specified as the use of religious language in a secular age, or as self-understanding, or as the supposed requirements of a scientific outlook, it is always falsely implied that no view of Christianity is possible for modern man other than one screened through empirical categories. But in fact the transcendent, supernatural God disclosed in the Judeo-Christian revelation in no way competes with what the modern man knows. The modern problem is not the transcendent God but rebellious man—not *modern* man in some peculiar way but *man* as fallen. Even in our time we are not dealing with a man who is wholly "godless," although we are dealing assuredly with a man who is *ungodly,* with a creature in the grip of sin and death for whom sin and death are such inescapable concerns that he resorts to the most ingenious devices—existential, linguistic, and secularistic—to becloud their existence. Because theological renegades ask the wrong question—How transform Christianity to enlist the secular man?—they come up with the perverse answer: Restructure the Gospel! rather than *Regenerate the sinner!* Instead of proclaiming God's revelation and demanding man's reconstruction, they enthrone secular empiricism and reconstitute the Christian religion.

The secular modern man fashions ingenious intellectual shelters to shield himself from divine confrontation and to hide himself from divine scrutiny and exposure. Much of the popular reading of our day, as well as some technical literature, mirrors man's spiritual evasion and equivocation, his moral ambiguity, his self-compromise in the face of ultimate concerns. The theological faddists provide a tidy formula capable of easy memorization and useful as a "shocker" by modern Athenians ever on the prowl for something new, always suspicious of a faith "once for all delivered to the saints," and therefore incapable of finding an intellectual resting-place. In hushed tones they impart the latest secret of the cosmos: "Christian faith is gone; Christian hope is gone; all that is left is Christian love —but that's enough."

To a generation dangling over the abyss of despair, any rope, however slim, is welcome. If *agape* can bear the burden of late twentieth-century doubt and anxiety, then *agape* is perhaps worth a try. If the supernatural and transcendent must go, if the historical is all that is left, especially the example of Jesus, perhaps that will patch up our raveling existence, even if this "agape" at times overtly justifies what the divine commandments and Jesus of Nazareth disapprove. It is not the inner logic of this proposal, nor any sound reason for such a hope, but the dire futility and emptiness of modern life that shapes a bare interest in this possibility —and, for that matter, in a hundred and one other contemporary cults. The linguistic theologians never tell us why human life *ought* to hold together; nor *why* Jesus alone holds it together; nor that this religious belief is objectively true; nor why it is logically superior to a contrary view. Nor can they.

A tired band of religious hopefuls, vulnerable victims of the biases of modernity, may rally momentarily to this expedient to justify their specialization in religion or their interest in the Church. But few college students are won to Christian faith by the modern proposals, which elevate the dated prejudices of the modern mind into status symbols and conform even the revelation of God and the Gospel of Christ to them. The man in the street and the layman in the pew shun such appeals because men desire truth no less than emotional satisfaction and cultural acceptance. None of the non-metaphysical theologies from Barth to Bultmann to Tillich to Robinson has nourished any great revival of lay interest in the Christian religion.

Back in the early 1950s Homrighausen noted that despite its emphasis on dynamic relevancy, the entire "Word of God" movement in contemporary theology has failed to produce a single evangelist. How irrelevant to the Great Commission can theologians get? Where do modern men—and there are multitudes of them—flock around Bultmann or Tillich or the linguistic theologians or the "death of God" theologians, crying out: "You have restored authentic Christianity to us!" The captive theological students in ecumenically minded seminaries are their main "converts"—Tillich made Tillichians at Harvard, Hamilton makes Hamiltonians at Colgate Rochester, Van Buren makes Van Burenites at Duke, Altizer makes Altizerites at Emory, and Loomer will be making Loomerites at Berkeley Baptist. But modern men hungry for spiritual reality will not be flocking there. They will fill up the Los Angeles Coliseum, or Madison Square Garden, and the other huge modern arenas to hear Billy Graham preach the New Testament evangel—and they give Graham a hearing in Europe and Africa no less than in North America and Latin America. Those who are always revising the Gospel to protect its power to persuade modern men seem curiously to leave the hard-core secularists as unpersuaded as ever, and to prepare the way for another reconstruction of their own theology a few years hence.

The great modern tragedy is not the problem of the man in the street. It is the spectacle of the theologian who assures him that he can repudiate supernaturalism, and that he *must* do so, to become a Christian. This sad development means not "the death of God" but the death of Protestant theology, however ecumenically respectable it may be.

RESTRICTION OF KNOWLEDGE

A decade ago Frederick Copleston warned of the emergence of a skeptical type of mind that spontaneously regards theology and metaphysics as "dreams and moonshine" and that is " 'naturally' closed to the Transcendent."[2] Today that skepticism has overtaken an ecclesiastically entrenched vanguard of pseudotheologians disposed to restrict valid knowledge to the world of nature and to man as described by the sciences. Whatever criticism empirical scientism offers of the Christian religion and of the Bible, these pseudotheologians accept; they no longer know what it is to contemplate the higher criticism of the prevailing philosophy of science. But it is precisely the contemporary theological reluctance to probe the possibility of attaining knowledge of transcendent reality and the significance of cognitive reasoning in religious experience that is the crucial neglected theological issue of our century.

While theologians dismiss cognitive knowledge of God, they remain intellectually powerless to compete with the sensate-empirical outlook of the modern age— whether they appeal to faith, to experience, to intuition, or to dialectical or existential varieties of "revelation." Alasdair MacIntyre considers Tillich and Bultmann atheists, because these guiding theologians of Robinson's *Honest to God* reject a literal objectifiable theism.[3] Yet MacIntyre himself, bypassing the "death of God" stop on the expressway from theism to atheism, goes to the end of the line. Karl Barth was surely right in saying that the distance was not great from the domain of Tillich and Bultmann to that of Feuerbach, but he was profoundly wrong in thinking that the mansions of dialectical theology were securely located in the suburbs of supernatural theism.

If Christianity is to win intellectual respectability in the modern world, the reality of the transcendent God must indeed be proclaimed by the theologians—and

[2]Frederick Copleston, *Contemporary Philosophy* (London: Burns, Oates, and Washbourne, 1956), p. 32.
[3]Alasdair MacIntyre, "God and the Theologians," *Encounter,* Sept., 1963.

proclaimed on the basis of man's rational competence to know the transempirical realm. Apart from recognition of the rational Creator of men made in his image and of the self-revealed Redeemer of a fallen humanity, who vouchsafes valid knowledge of the transempirical world, the modern Athenians are left to munch the husks of the religious vagabonds.

Index

PERSONS

156

SUBJECTS